INTERNATIONAL BUSINESS LAW

Bilingual Teaching Case

国际商法
双语教学案例

主　编　白泉旺

副主编　朱福建

北京大学出版社

PEKING UNIVERSITY PRESS

内 容 简 介

本书是"国际商法"课程教学辅助用书，在体系上与主流国际商法教材保持一致。本书突出"以案说法"，充分发挥与教材相辅相成的作用。全书共 35 个案例，涵盖了国际商法的基本理论、基本规则与基本内容，涉及跨国公司全球战略、跨国公司社会责任、跨国直接投资、国际商事合同，以及国际货物运输和国际贸易支付等方面的国际商事规则与规范。

本书适用于国际商务专业、国际贸易专业及国际工商管理专业的本科生使用，同时也可供相关领域从业人员参考。

图书在版编目（CIP）数据

国际商法：双语教学案例 / 白泉旺主编 . —北京：北京大学出版社，2023.1
ISBN 978-7-301-33603-8

Ⅰ . ①国… Ⅱ . ①白… Ⅲ . ①国际商法—教案（教育）—高等学校 Ⅳ . ① D996.1

中国版本图书馆 CIP 数据核字（2022）第 217509 号

书　　　名	国际商法：双语教学案例
	GUOJI SHANGFA：SHUANGYU JIAOXUE ANLI
著作责任者	白泉旺　主编
策 划 编 辑	李娉婷
责 任 编 辑	耿　哲　李娉婷
标 准 书 号	ISBN 978-7-301-33603-8
出 版 发 行	北京大学出版社
地　　　址	北京市海淀区成府路 205 号　　100871
网　　　址	http：//www.pup.cn　　　新浪微博：@ 北京大学出版社
电 子 邮 箱	编辑部 pup6@pup.cn　　　总编室 zpup@pup.cn
电　　　话	邮购部 010-62752015　　发行部 010-62750672　　编辑部 010-62750667
印 刷 者	天津和萱印刷有限公司
经 销 者	新华书店
	787 毫米 × 1092 毫米　16 开本　13.75 印张　218 千字
	2023 年 1 月第 1 版　　2025 年 6 月第 2 次印刷
定　　　价	59.00 元

前　　言

随着经济全球化的深入发展，国际经济活动呈现出两个明显的特征：一是国际经济的融合性；二是国际商事规则的统一性。国际商事主体在重视全球战略和国际市场拓展的同时，更加重视自身的社会责任，重视其在国际投资、国际贸易、国际金融和国际税收等领域中的合规性。"国际商法"作为一门全面系统地介绍国际商事主体，以及国际投资规则、国际贸易规则及国际金融规则等国际商事活动规则的课程，其在培养复合型商科人才方面的重要性日益凸显。同时，与"国际商法"相应的配套教材和案例的编写、运用也具有举足轻重的作用。在宁波大学工商管理专业国际化建设的推动下，本书编者结合近年来讲授"国际商法"的实践，尝试编译了本书。

本书是一本教学辅助用书，编写遵循学以致用、深入浅出的原则。在体系上，本书与主流国际商法教材基本一致，突出"以案说法"的特点，并发挥与教材相辅相成的作用；在结构上，各案例包含案例介绍、案例分析和结论等重点模块；在内容编排上，本书涉及国际商法的基本规则、规范及规定。希望学生通过阅读本书，能更好地掌握国际商法的基本理论、基本知识和基本规则。

本书共有三十五个案例。其中，与跨国公司全球战略相关的案例有四个，与跨国公司社会责任相关的案例有五个，与跨国直接投资相关的案例有八个，与国际商事合同相关的案例有六个，与国际货物运输相关的案例有六个，与国际贸易支付相关的案例有六个。为了兼顾国内学生和留学生的学习，以上三十五个案例分别配有中英文版本。

实践证明，借助案例教学环节，可以深化学生对"国际商法"课堂教学内容的理解。在此，特别感谢本书中案例的原作者，正是这些前辈和同人的开拓和指引，才使得我们的课堂教学内容有了丰富的素材。需要说明的是，本书在案例选用过程中，出于教学需要和编写规范，在不改变案例主体思想的基础上对一些案例内容进行了适当的调整和补充。另外，在案例翻译过程中，编者主观上希望用通俗的语言去表达法律中一些晦涩的术语，所以译文中的个别句子可能缺少地道的法律语言"味道"。

本书的顺利出版得益于宁波大学商学院工商管理系的支持，在此表示感谢。此外，还要感谢彭新敏教授和国维潇博士的督促，感谢北京大学出版社耿哲编辑细致和耐心的帮助！

白泉旺　朱福建

宁波大学

2022 年 7 月

Preface

International economic activities show two distinct features with the deep development of economic globalization: the international economy becomes more integrated and international business rules get more united. While focusing on their global strategies and development in global market, the entities engaged in international businesses attach more importance to their social responsibilities and their compliance with the rules and norms regarding international investment, international trade, international finance and international taxation. International Business Laws is an important course that introduces international bussiness entities and the rules of international business activities comprehensively and systematically, including international investments, international trade, and international finance. The compilation, application of supporting textbooks and cases for International Business Law are very important. Driven by the development of internationalization of Business Administration Major in Ningbo University, we prepared this book based on our experiences in the teaching of International Business Law bilingually or in English in recent years.

This book may be used as supporting materials for teaching activities. It is drafted in the practice-oriented principle and easy-to-understand approach. The book is systematically consistent, correlated, and complementary with the textbook of International Business Law. Each case consists of three parts: case description, case analysis, and conclusion. The content of the cases covers the basic international business laws and rules. By reading the cases, the students are expected to get a clear understanding of the basic theories and knowledge of international business laws.

The book contains thirty-five cases among which four cases are regarding the global strategy of international corporations, five regarding the social responsibility of international corporations, eight regarding international direct investment, six regarding international business contracts, six regarding international cargo transportation and the other six regarding international trade payment. All cases are drafted in both Chinese and English.

Practices show that case-based teaching is helpful for the students to understand the content of international business laws given in classroom teaching. We would like to express our appreciation for the writers of the cases. They provided abundant materials for our classroom teaching. It should be noted that for the translation of these cases, although the translators have made efforts to translate the cases in an easy-to-understand way, some legal terms and expressions in the law are difficult to understand and possibly the translations are not native.

At the moment of publication of this book, we would like to express our thanks for the support given by the Department of Business Administration of Ningbo University, Professor Peng Xinmin and Dr. Guo Weixiao, and especially Geng Zhe, editor of Peking University Press, who carried out lots of work carefully and patiently for the publication of the book.

Bai Quanwang

Zhu Fujian

Ningbo University

July 2022

目　　录

第 *1* 章

跨国公司全球化战略

1.1　BP 公司在美战略规划

【知识点】

跨国公司、战略规划、国际生产折中理论

【案例介绍】

英国石油公司（BP）是一家主导全球石油工业的跨国公司。BP 具备区位优势，并拥有资金、技术、企业管理、市场营销等方面的所有权优势。同时，借助于一体化的整合能力，BP 的内部化优势在跨国经营过程中也得到充分展现。从油田开采到最终生产出石化产品的整个生产链中，BP 所需的中间产品都可以通过内部交易获得。但在早期的跨国经营中，BP 的业务主要集中在中东的石油生产和西欧的石化产品生产方面，全球化程度不高，尤其在美国市场处于劣势地位。美国所具有的区位优势，如稳定的政治环境、活跃的私人企业文化、巨大的市场容量和较高的产品利润率，使其成为世界石油企业最理想的投资目标国。

1958 年，BP 拟通过与辛克莱石油公司的合作打开美国市场，但由于美国当时实施强制性石油进口配额使得其他国家对美国的石油出口受到限制，因此此次合作没有达到预期效果。1969 年，美国普拉德霍湾地区发现了巨大的石油储量，BP 再一次看到了在美国投资的机会。不过，BP 想在美国市场发展还有几个问题需要解决：第一，BP 必须在美国建立自己的石油生产与经营的垂直网络；第二，要尽快掌握在美国进行大规模经营的市场经验和管理能力；第三，要解决美国当时对其国内能源市场的保护问题。因此，BP 决定利用美国本土企业（俄亥俄标准石油公司）进入美国市场。俄亥俄标准石油公司作为目标公司的优势在于：第一，其核心业务即石油冶炼和石化产品销售，在美国市场份额中位列第四；第二，该公司拥有很强的管理能力和资金实力，具备进一步开拓市场的能力；第三，该公司股东分散，便于 BP 获得控制权；第四，该公司缺乏石油储备。因此，BP 在上游产品的所有权优势与俄亥俄标准石油公司在下游产品的所有权优势，构成了双方开展优势互补的合作的基础。

【案例分析】

本案例介绍了 BP 进入美国市场的战略，这些战略思想和内容体现了跨国公司全球化战略的基本特征。下面我们从前期战略规划和后期战略整合两方面对案例进行分析。

1. 前期战略规划

1970 年年初，BP 将其阿拉斯加油田的大部分股份及部分辛克莱石油公司下游资产转让给俄亥俄标准石油公司，从而获得其原始股。根据当时的政策，如果 BP 过多插手俄亥俄标准石油公司业务，会与美国法律相抵触，因为在美国小股东的权益受到的法律保护更多，因此 BP 仍保持了俄亥俄标准石油公司的独立性。另外，保持相互独立还可避免因违反谢尔曼法而遭到惩罚。根据谢尔曼法，任何限制竞争的合并及共谋均视为违法，双方之间如果存在着股权关联关系，它们就可能在价格等市场行为中形成共谋，这种行为就会违反美国法律。因此，此次并购使 BP 的所有权优势和区位优势都得以发挥，但因并购双方协议的限制，BP 的内部化优势难以得到有效发挥。

2. 后期战略整合

在并购早期，双方的利益汇合点主要是在普拉德霍湾的石油开采上，虽然没有充分发挥出 BP 的内部化优势，但巨大的石油储量使双方都获得了大量的利润。20 世纪 70 年代末，随着俄亥俄标准石油公司在全球经营中的地位越来越高，BP 参与其公司经营管理的愿望与日俱增，希望能将其作为控股的子公司进行必要整合，并将其纳入 BP 的全球整体规划中。但俄亥俄标准石油公司认为，如果 BP 作为大股东参与管理，可能会侵犯少数小股东的合法权益，会造成俄亥俄标准石油公司原有员工的不满，因此依然保持自身较强的独立性。20 世纪 80 年代中期，由于美国逐渐开放石油进口，因此美国市场的战略利益对 BP 来说越来越重要，俄亥俄标准石油公司也随之成为集团中最重要的子公司。BP 决定进行全面收购和整合，更换了俄亥俄标准石油公司的管理层，但由于担心美国法律对小股东的保护，因此仍保持了俄亥俄标准石油公司的独立性。直至 1987 年，BP 才完成了对俄亥俄标准石油公司剩余股份的收购，并获得了全面控制权，随后开始对其进行有效整合。BP 通过其在美国境内外企业的内部化优势，实现了公司在全球的发展战略。

【结论】

BP 的国际化经营动因与国际生产折中理论是相符的。BP 对俄亥俄标准石油公司进一步的整合并购更多地体现在利益共享、技术与知识共享，以及更高程度地发挥集团的内部化优势等方面，而这些对 BP 在全球的战略经营都发挥了重要作用，极大地提高了 BP 在全球能源市场中的地位。

【案例来源】

陈顺长.跨国并购案例分析及其对中国的启示[D].北京：北京交通大学，2007.

【案例问题】

（1）BP 在美国的战略规划及其核心内容是什么？

（2）BP 在制订战略规划时会面临哪些法律问题？

1.2　万达集团在美战略实施

【知识点】

企业国际化、跨国并购、战略目标、战略实施

【案例介绍】

2012 年 5 月 21 日，万达集团与全球第二大院线集团美国 AMC 影院（以下简称 AMC）正式签署了并购协议，以 31 亿美元（包括并购的总交易金额 26 亿美元及并购后投入 AMC 的不超过 5 亿美元的营运资金）购买 AMC 100% 的股权，并承担 AMC 的相关债务。

【案例分析】

本案例主要介绍了万达集团成功并购 AMC 的事件。站在双方各自的角度观察这一案例时，可以发现他们各自的战略目标十分清晰，具体如下。

1. 万达的战略目标

2005 年，万达集团开始投资文化产业，并成立万达院线。2010 年，万达集团制订了在文化产业上实现跨国发展的十年战略目标。并购 AMC 就是万达集团实现这一目标的重要举措之一。首先，万达集团对 AMC 进行了详细和全面的评估与考察，选择并购 AMC 是万达集团文化产业走向国际化的第一步。如果并购成功，万达集团可以扩大其业务的经营范围，并且通过 AMC 的资源和渠道，与更多有名的电影公司合作。其次，通过并购，万达集团可以以最少的资金进入美国市场，并取得最大的利益。最后，由于 AMC 与万达集团的电影资源和资金流可以共享，所以双方都能够提高公司的财务收入，实现资金流的稳定增长。从长期来看，万达集团可以凭借并购 AMC 减少自身的经营风险，提高在美国市场的竞争力。

2. AMC 的战略目标

受经济危机影响，美国院线业竞争加剧，电影业业绩不断下滑，票房持续下降，加上自身经营不善，AMC 陷入亏损和巨额债务负担的双重困境。其公司年报显示，截至 2012 年 3 月底，AMC 亏损额度高达 8200 万美元，其总资产为 36.38 亿美元，负债为 34.84 亿美元，负债率达 96%。可见，AMC 维持自身的运营已经十分艰难，因此 AMC 的主要控股者有了将其出售的意愿，而这为万达集团的并购计划创造了有利的时机。

【结论】

万达集团通过企业国际化战略实现了自己的战略目标。AMC 通过与万达集团结合，缓解了当时 AMC 负债累累的情况，对 AMC 来说，这也是一个正确的战略决策。双方达到了双赢的目的。

【案例来源】

[1] 蔡雨欣.中国企业赴美并购案例分析[J].中国经贸导刊（中），2019（7）：58-59.

[2] 李萌.大连万达集团并购美国 AMC 的案例分析[D].兰州：兰州财经大学，2015.

【案例问题】

万达集团能够成功进入美国市场的战略是什么？

1.3　英博公司在华战略布局

【知识点】

跨国并购、股权转让、战略布局

【案例介绍】

自 2001 年起，雪津啤酒通过规模和品牌扩张，逐步完成了从产品经营到品牌经营再到资本经营的跳跃式发展。随着中国经济的持续发展，人民生活水平的不断提高，中国啤酒市场迎来了巨大的发展机遇，世界啤酒巨头企业纷纷涌入中国市场。当时的雪津啤酒在考察了哈尔滨、重庆等地的啤酒企业后，决定将国有股权和非国有股权捆绑出售，其目的在于方便收购者绝对控股，从而吸引更多竞争者参与竞购，拉升成交价格。

2005年6月中旬，雪津啤酒聘请普华永道为财务顾问，2005年7月底，双方共同商讨雪津啤酒股权的转让事宜，最终作出以下决定：①雪津啤酒股权转让采取场内交易方式，由福建省产权交易中心挂牌出让雪津啤酒国有股权，竞购者初步圈定国际前四大啤酒巨头和国内前三大啤酒公司；②采取"两轮竞标"的招投标方案，第一轮招投标主要筛选竞标者，第二轮招投标为正式竞标及确定最终报价；③本次收购的前提是坚持"四不变"原则，即股权受让人必须保证雪津啤酒"注册地不变""纳税地不变""品牌不变""管理层和员工基本不变"。

2005年12月7日，第二轮竞价在福建省产权交易中心举行。只有一家来自比利时的英博公司参加竞价，最后以58.86亿元报价成交。

2006年1月23日，位于比利时的英博公司总部正式宣布，将以58.86亿元的价格分两阶段收购雪津啤酒全部股权，将先以23.24亿元买下雪津啤酒39.48%的国有股权，然后于2007年年底以35.62亿元收购雪津啤酒剩下的60.52%的非国有股权。在之后的一个月里，英博公司与雪津啤酒进行了具体谈判，确定了股权转让的详细条款。最终，双方签署了共25项收购协议。其中有3份协议最为重要，包括《股权收购协议》《保持纳税地不变的协议》《承诺不做结构性裁员的协议》。

【案例分析】

本案例聚焦比利时英博公司对中国雪津啤酒的收购，二者之间的互动形成了正和博弈，其结果是参与各方均受益。

1. 雪津啤酒受益

雪津啤酒获得的好处至少有以下几个。①股东权益增值。雪津啤酒以净资产6亿多元的估值，卖出58.86亿元的天价，净资产溢价率高达1000%。②实现了企业的可持续发展且保护了民族品牌。根据双方协议，股权转让后，英博公司"不能限制雪津啤酒的发展空间",也"不能限制雪津啤酒品牌的扩张",必须长期持有雪津啤酒的股份,必须利用母公司优势提升雪津啤酒的国际市场地位。③稳定了就业和管理团队。协议规定,英博公司受让雪津啤酒股份后,在规定时间内,不得进行结构性裁员,不得更换企业管理团队,同时必须逐步采取与国际接轨的激励机制。

2. 地方政府受益

雪津啤酒的所在地福建省莆田市在此次交易中也是受益方。①实现引资新突破。从雪津啤酒转让中获得 8 亿元收入。②实现社会效益最大化。雪津啤酒坚持"注册地不变""纳税地不变""品牌不变"等原则,不仅能够确保雪津啤酒对地方财政收入的贡献不减,还可以提升雪津啤酒和莆田市的国际形象。

3. 英博公司受益

英博公司在此次交易中也是受益方。英博公司亚太法律与企业事务副总裁认为,英博公司收购雪津啤酒,不仅是一笔超值的收购,而且是英博公司完成战略布局、扩大市场版图和谋求整体效益必不可少的环节。

【结论】

中国持续扩大对外开放,为越来越多的外国投资者提供了良好的投资机遇。收购雪津啤酒是英博公司的成功案例之一,也是其实现规模经济和全球布局的一个战略决策。

【案例来源】

任永菊.跨国公司与对外直接投资[M].北京:清华大学出版社,2019.

【案例问题】

英博公司在中国完成其战略布局体现出跨国公司的哪些特征?

1.4　苹果公司在华战略选择

【知识点】

跨国公司、全球战略、本土化策略、战略选择

【案例介绍】

美国苹果公司，原名苹果电脑公司，后于 2007 年更名为苹果公司，是世界上最大的 IT 科技企业之一，也是全球第一大手机生产商。目前，在全球经营最成功的几家电子产品企业中，苹果公司是当之无愧的佼佼者。其手机能在全世界范围畅销，除了因为它具有产品外观、质量、性能方面的优势，其公司的经营策略也是非常重要的。

【案例分析】

本案例简要介绍了苹果公司。关于苹果公司的经营战略及战略内涵，需要结合战略理论中的优势方面和劣势方面加以分析。

1. 苹果公司的优势

（1）产品优势。

首先，苹果手机有特殊的工艺设计，给消费者提供了优良的触感、美观的外形，产品易于使用，且看起来很高级，与普通品牌手机有着明显的差异。其次，苹果手机具有独一无二的 iOS 系统。iOS 系统保证了苹果手机高度的易用性和便捷性，且之后的开发、升级和修复也简单很多。最后，苹果公司也在不断创新，特别是近几年来围绕客户需求进行创新，切实为客户开发新产品，赢得了更多客户的追捧。

（2）品牌知名度。

根据历年美国《福布斯》公布的全球品牌价值排行榜，科技巨头苹果公司已经

连续多年夺冠，特别是 2019 年，苹果公司的品牌价值达到了 2055 亿美元，比上年增长了 12%，同时这也是第一次有品牌的价值突破 2000 亿美元。品牌的价值与企业的发展息息相关，各企业的发展模式不可能相同，每个企业都有其独一无二的发展方式，这就使得苹果公司的品牌在长期内很难被模仿和代替。

（3）重视研发。

苹果公司是一家自己生产硬件和软件的科技公司，它拥有强大的研发力量，非常重视先进技术的研发工作。从第一代到第十代手机，苹果公司分别研发了全触控屏幕、多点触屏、视网膜屏幕、前置摄像头、视频通话、背面玻璃、无线充电、面部识别等一系列在当时既先进又独特的技术。苹果公司的产品设计一直都是一流的，并且常常会让市场在某一方面发生革命性的改变，苹果公司的新产品还常常被其他企业模仿。

2. 苹果公司的劣势

（1）价格偏高。

苹果手机的定位是高端产品，其价格越来越高，而且可选择性有限，无法满足不同消费者的需求。一部苹果手机的价格相当于一台质量不错的笔记本电脑，其昂贵的价格容易使消费者望而止步，而当人们感觉不到物有所值时，就会考虑选择其他品牌的手机。

（2）供应链不完善。

一些很关键的零件会出现供应不足的现象，苹果公司在应对这种市场需求突变的情况时会表现乏力，进而失去竞争力。例如，苹果电脑的显示屏供应商很少，而苹果公司又有很高的技术规格要求，所以找替代品会很难，当供应商提供的产品出现问题时，就可能会出现延期交货的情况。

（3）售后服务存在不足。

虽然苹果手机在中国很受欢迎，但是它的售后服务仍然有待改进。根据 2012 年中国消费者协会的统计，在用户对苹果手机的投诉中，售后服务占 25.6%。

【结论】

苹果公司的成功有其自身的科技实力支撑，也有其经营管理方面一系列策略的支持。作为跨国公司，苹果公司在中国的经营战略应注重发挥自身的产品优势、品牌优势和研发优势，做好价格定位，优化供应链和售后服务，不断满足中国消费者的需求，只有这样做才能取得持续良好的业绩。

【案例来源】

罗欣，刘艳利．苹果公司战略选择[J].合作经济与科技，2021（7）：116-117.

【案例问题】

苹果公司在中国的战略选择对中国企业海外本土化经营有哪些借鉴意义？

第 2 章

跨国公司社会责任

2.1 谷歌在欧盟市场的垄断

【知识点】

跨国公司、市场垄断、市场支配地位、滥用市场支配地位

【案例介绍】

2017 年 6 月，欧盟委员会认为谷歌滥用其在搜索引擎市场的支配地位来为自己的比较购物服务提供非法优势地位，这种滥用市场支配地位的行为，应当受到反垄断法的规制，因此欧盟委员会最终决定对谷歌罚款 24.2 亿欧元。2021 年 11 月，欧盟普通法院维持了这一判决。

比较购物服务是谷歌的专门搜索服务之一，该服务根据用户查询从商家网站获取产品报价，从而使用户可以对各个商家的价格进行比较，商家无须付费即可在搜索结果中被列出。此外，搜索结果可能还会显示由谷歌旗下的 AdWords 投放的在线搜索广告，AdWords 的搜索结果可由任何广告商购买。

【案例分析】

本案例主要涉及谷歌在欧盟市场的垄断行为。根据欧盟有关市场运行条例，欧盟对企业滥用市场支配地位和垄断行为的认定主要是从以下方面展开的。

1. 企业获得市场支配地位

界定市场支配地位的一个重要因素是企业占有较大比例的市场份额。欧盟委员会发现，自 2008 年以来，谷歌搜索引擎在欧洲经济区国家占据了 90% 以上的市场份额，而其最主要的竞争对手之一"必应"占据的市场份额却小于 5%。根据欧盟法院判例，企业市场份额达到 70% ～ 80% 即可确定为占据市场支配地位。由此推

定谷歌在搜索引擎市场占据支配地位。另外，免费提供服务的事实也是评估支配地位时要考虑的一个相关因素。

2. 企业有滥用市场支配地位的行为

谷歌在其一般搜索结果页面中突出显示了自己的比较购物服务。尽管竞争性比较购物服务只能显示为一般搜索结果，并且能够通过某些算法使其他网站在搜索结果页面中的排名降低。但谷歌对自己的比较购物服务给予了突出显示的待遇，并且通过算法设置使其永远不会因其他网站的算法而被降低排名。这是典型的滥用市场支配地位和排挤竞争对手、破坏市场竞争秩序的行为。

3. 企业在数字经济活动中的行为

在谷歌垄断案中，虽然市场份额是欧盟委员会认定谷歌具有市场支配地位的主要因素，但在确认谷歌滥用市场支配地位的行为时，欧盟委员会不仅考虑了网络外部效应对构成市场壁垒的影响力，还分析了谷歌操纵算法将自己的比较购物网站显示在搜索结果前列的行为。

【结论】

数字经济对滥用市场支配地位的认定提出了挑战，尤其表现在以下三个方面：①相关市场界定困难；②滥用市场支配地位的行为比较复杂；③滥用市场支配地位的行为具有隐蔽性。因此，在数字经济时代，应当充分认清数字经济的特点，再结合互联网行业特征进行反垄断规制分析，与时俱进，从而达到保护市场竞争的目的。

【案例来源】

[1] 赵晨芳. 数字经济时代互联网企业反垄断的挑战与应对：由"谷歌利用算法滥用支配地位"案切入[J]. 长春市委党校学报，2019（2）：35-40.

[2] 杨坚琪. 谷歌在欧洲：欧盟运行条约（TFEU）第 102 条视角下的谷歌垄断行为分析[J]. 竞争政策研究，2017（1）：56-78.

【案例问题】

结合国际商法中有关国际投资法的内容，试说明东道国应如何规制跨国公司的垄断行为。

2.2 日本高田"气囊"责任

【知识点】

跨国公司、产品责任、消费者权益保护

【案例介绍】

日本高田创立于 1933 年，是一家专门生产汽车安全气囊、方向盘、安全带、电子感应装置及其他汽车安全零配件的跨国公司，总部设在日本东京。高田公司为丰田、三菱、宝马等众多汽车制造商提供安全气囊，最辉煌时曾占据全球安全气囊市场 22% 的份额，是当时全球三大安全气囊制造商之一。

2009 年 5 月 16 日，美国一位 18 岁的女孩儿开着一辆 2000 年生产的本田雅阁与另一辆车相撞。气囊展开后，女孩被气囊中弹出的一块金属划破颈动脉，最终女孩失血而亡。随后，高田的气囊缺陷问题进入公众视野。

2019 年之前，在全球范围内，因高田气囊导致的安全事件至少造成 23 人死亡，数百人受伤。媒体公布的数据显示，截至 2017 年 5 月，全球因装配问题气囊而被召回的缺陷汽车总量高达 1.2 亿辆，牵扯其中的汽车品牌包括奔驰、宝马、福特、大众、通用、丰田、日产、特斯拉等 19 家车企，几乎涉及了所有主流汽车品牌。2017年，与高田合作的汽车品牌商召回了问题车辆并实施了相应的补偿方案，同时对高田提出巨额诉讼赔偿要求。在这些案件中，除了高额的费用外，高田还要进行人身伤害赔偿。高田 2016 年的财务报告显示，高田销售额为 6625 亿日元，亏损则高达

795 亿日元。此外，高田还要向全球主要汽车厂商赔付 8.5 亿美元。2017 年 6 月 26 日，高田公司向东京地方法院申请破产保护，同时其在美国的核心子公司"TK 控股"也向当地法院申请了破产保护。2018 年，我国因高田气囊问题被召回的车辆总数超过 170 万辆，占当年汽车召回总量的 14.19%。2019 年，斯巴鲁、特斯拉、宝马、大众、戴姆勒卡货车、奔驰、法拉利等多家汽车制造商对装配了高田问题气囊的车辆启动了新一轮召回。

【案例分析】

本案例主要介绍了日本高田生产的汽车安全气囊存在产品缺陷及由此产生的严重影响与后果。

高田的汽车安全气囊有严重的产品缺陷。高田在生产的气囊中安装了气体推进剂，这原本是为了在汽车发生碰撞时，气囊能够更快速地弹出。然而这个推进剂被装在了一块金属中，这块细小的金属在汽车发生碰撞的情况下会自动弹出来。同时，为了降低成本，高田公司在气体发生器中使用了硝酸铵。该原料在保存不当的情况下就会受潮变质，极易引起气体发生器爆炸，而爆炸时迸射的碎片就会对前排乘客造成安全威胁。高田气囊在近十年的时间里，造成多起严重的交通事故，导致二十多人死亡，数百人受伤。消费者不仅人身受到伤害，还要花费大量的钱财进行后续维护，如购买新的汽车安全气囊，甚至购买新的汽车，有时还会涉及大额的医疗费用。此外，因高田气囊导致的死亡，给那些失去亲人的家庭带来了长期的痛苦。作为罪魁祸首的高田，不仅要对那些合作的汽车公司进行巨额赔偿，还要对发生事故的消费者的家庭进行赔偿，赔偿金额高达几十亿元人民币。最终，高田公司及其在美国的子公司因承受不了巨额赔款，于 2017 年宣布破产。

汽车安全非常重要。汽车的安全系统主要包括安全气囊和安全带。此前，美国高速公路安全管理局调查结果显示，正确使用安全气囊可减少 11% 的汽车驾驶员死亡率和降低 30% 的正面撞击力。可以说，车辆如果在行驶中发生碰撞，安全气囊可以减轻车内人员的受伤害程度，最大限度地保护车内人员的生命安全。

作为一个跨国公司，日本高田公司曾经是全球三大安全气囊制造商之一，占全球安全气囊市场份额的五分之一，在美国拥有子公司，且与多家知名汽车品牌有合作往来，因此，高田气囊事件涉及了众多知名汽车名牌，对他们的声誉造成了一定的负面影响，给车企及消费者都带来了无法挽回的损失。可见，汽车生产商应该投入更多的精力和财力，提高产品质量，否则，一旦发生危险，那就是致命的。

全球采购具有弊端。如今全球的汽车生产都是通过全球采购来实现的，如购买日本的安全气囊、购买德国的轮胎等，因为这样能够大幅降低成本，从而使企业获得更多的利润，但同时带来的问题也是显而易见的。当然，从单一公司采购也有弊端，如从单一公司采购汽车零件会造成该公司对汽车零件市场的垄断，而使其他竞争公司陷入困境。如果过于依赖单一公司的汽车零件，那么一旦该公司出现无法交单的情况，汽车销售商就必须配合其零件供应商的进度而对自己的生产进度安排做出调整。另外，如果大量从单一汽车零件公司购买产品，那么该零件公司为了赚取更多的利益，可能会降低成本，从而导致产品质量下降，并造成更严重的危险。

因产品责任产生的问题具有严重性、持久性等特征。高田气囊事件始于2009年，直到2019年，每年仍有上百万辆汽车因高田气囊问题被召回，潜在的危险仍然存在，驾驶员在汽车行驶时不仅要面对道路上的危险，还要仔细检查汽车零件是否存在问题，因此车企应以高田气囊事件为鉴，直面问题、改进技术，从而在激烈的市场竞争中立于不败之地。

【结论】

日本高田气囊事件引发了人们对汽车安全的担忧，也使消费者对一些跨国公司产品的信任度降低。日本高田虽然破产了，但该事件留给人们的教训却是深刻的。根据多数国家的产品责任法及实施规则，当产品缺陷导致产品的消费者、使用者或第三者发生财产损失或人身伤害时，产品的生产商或销售商应共同承担赔偿责任。

【案例来源】

［1］闫欣雨.透视"高田气囊门"［N］.新京报，2015-06-29（B17）.

［2］王亚菲.高田"死亡气囊"事件即将以破产告终［N］.新京报，2017-07-03（B12）.

【案例问题】

试比较普通法系和大陆法系对产品责任的界定。

2.3 威士伯涂料污染事件

【知识点】

跨国公司、环境污染、企业社会责任

【案例介绍】

2018年7月17日，上海市嘉定区环境保护局公开一则行政处罚：威士伯涂料（上海）有限公司因环境违法（含挥发性有机物废气未按规定使用污染防治设施、无组织排放），上海市嘉定区环境保护局依据《中华人民共和国大气污染防治法》第45条和第108条第一款第一项规定对其予以行政处罚，罚款金额为10万元。

威士伯涂料（上海）有限公司曾于2016年12月因环保违规行为被上海市嘉定区环境保护局以违反《中华人民共和国大气污染防治法》第45条规定处罚12万元，并责令立即改正，处罚事由是"产生含挥发性有机物废气的生产活动，未在密闭空间或者设备中进行"。做出行政处罚决定的日期为2016年12月20日。此后威士伯涂料（上海）有限公司又因违反污染防治管理制度被上海市嘉定区环境保护局处罚，处罚措施为"责令改正违法行为，并处罚款"，这一次处罚决定做出时间为 2017 年 1 月 10 日。2018 年 4 月 26 日，威士伯涂料（上海）有限公司因"含挥发性有机物废气未按规定使用污染防治设施、无组织排放"遭到上海市嘉定区环境保护局处罚，罚款金额为 7 万元。2019 年 7 月 2 日，威士伯涂料（上海）有限公司因"废气无组织排放"遭到上海市嘉定区生态环境局处罚，罚款金额为 7 万元。

【案例分析】

本案例主要介绍了威士伯涂料（上海）有限公司在生产过程中多次违反中国的环境保护法，受到上海市生态环境局行政处罚的情况。

美国威士伯成立于 1806 年，是世界第六大涂料制造商。该公司业务遍及全球 26 个国家，威士伯是全球卷钢表面涂料的领导者，也是中国家具漆市场的领导者。

威士伯涂料（上海）有限公司成立于 1999 年 10 月 20 日，注册资本为 1510 万美元，股东为"威士伯（亚洲）工业有限公司"，主要从事涂料、油漆、混合溶剂和混合添加剂的生产，销售本公司自产产品并为其产品提供售后服务和技术指导。

威士伯涂料（上海）有限公司属于跨国公司，该公司多次被上海市嘉定区生态环境局处罚，皆因违反了《中华人民共和国大气污染防治法》第 45 条和第 108 条。该公司数次被处罚却不进行整改，显示出公司社会责任感的严重缺失。在发达国家，由于排污标准苛刻，对超排的惩罚力度比较大，为了避免巨额罚金，企业往往会严格执行排污规定。因此有些跨国公司在其母国严格遵循绿色生产标准，控制污染水平，但在中国却漠视环保责任，为追求企业自身利益最大化而压缩成本，加剧了我国的环境污染。

近年来，跨国公司在华投资规模和投资数量不断扩大，仅 2018 年中国实际利用外资金额就高达 8856.1 亿元人民币，成为全球第二大外资流入国。大量外资企业的涌入，以及我国之前环保管理制度不完善的情况给我国带来了严峻的环境污染问题。虽然近年来，中国外资投资额增长速度有所放缓，但是由其带来的环境污染问题仍不容小觑。从跨国公司类型来看，在华投资的跨国公司以加工制造型跨国公司为主，占到所有跨国公司的三分之二，其次是资源开发型跨国公司和服务提供型跨国公司。

从行业结构来看，我国吸收的跨国直接投资主要集中在制造业，而制造业是产生污染物（尤其是废气污染）最严重的行业，很多制造业都属于污染密集型产业。这些污染密集型产业，主要是指在生产过程中若不加以治理就会直接或间接产生大量污染物的产业，这些污染物会对人类及动植物的生命健康造成严重的损害，会恶化环境、影响生态质量。

【结论】

中国应坚持发展绿色经济，加大政府监管力度，完善相关法律和制度，加大执法部门监督、检查力度，做到排污必究、执法必严、公平合理。同时，严格外资企业准入的绿色环保审核体系，严格执行准入标准，并建立和完善跨国公司在华履行企业社会责任的激励机制，鼓励跨国公司在华采取积极措施承担其企业责任，做到奖惩有度。

【案例来源】

吕邦皓，王兴.跨国公司在华投资环境污染问题及对策研究[J].今日财富（中国知识产权），2020（11）：8-9.

【案例问题】

试结合威士伯涂料污染事件，说明跨国公司履行社会责任的现实意义。

2.4 "加拿大鹅"虚假广告

【知识点】

外资企业、市场营销、虚假广告、不正当竞争

【案例介绍】

上海市黄浦区市场监督管理局对"加拿大鹅"（Canada Goose）关联公司希计（上海）商贸有限公司处以罚款45万元的行政处罚，原因是其利用广告对商品或服务做虚假宣传，欺骗和误导消费者。

"我们的所有羽绒混合材料均含有鹅羽绒，这是优良且最保暖的加拿大鹅绒……"动辄一件售价上万元的网红"加拿大鹅"品牌羽绒服，因这句虚假宣传语而"翻车"。其销售的大部分羽绒服并没有使用保温性能更出色的高蓬松度鹅绒，而是使用了蓬松度较低的鸭绒，因此当事人以偏概全地称其产品所使用的羽绒"优良且最保暖"与事实不符。

此外，联系到2020年"加拿大鹅"天猫旗舰店网页点击量达1.81亿次，销售额达人民币1.67亿元，可见涉案广告具有一定的社会影响。依据《中华人民共和国广告法》相关规定，市场监管部门决定对当事人依法处以罚款人民币45万元，责令其停止发布违法广告，并在相应范围内消除影响。

【案例分析】

这是一起在华外资企业损害消费者权益的案例，其主要行为是利用虚假广告误导消费者以谋取不当利益。

外资企业常凭借其"舶来品"的优越性受到推崇，产品价格更是频频出现天价。为吸引中国消费者，"加拿大鹅"更是大肆宣传其羽绒服的保暖性，用上了"最保暖"等绝对化字样，但是该公司却以质量较差的鸭绒充当质量更佳的鹅绒，违反了《中华人民共和国广告法》，构成虚假广告行为。

《中华人民共和国广告法》规定，发布广告不得使用"最高级""最佳"等绝对化字样。"加拿大鹅"利用消费者最看重的保暖性做虚假宣传，误导消费者，对市场中的同类型产品构成不当竞争，属于违法销售行为。

【结论】

合法销售是一家企业应该遵守的法律底线。不管是国内企业还是外资企业，进入一个市场就应该对这个市场的消费者负责，而不是通过非法手段欺骗消费者和挤占市场中同行业竞争者的生存空间来换取高额利润。

【案例来源】

张国栋.加拿大鹅广告"翻车"是虚假宣传的典型案例[N].中国质量报，2021-09-06（A04）.

【案例问题】

结合以上案例，试说明东道国应当如何有效规范跨国公司的不正当竞争行为。

2.5　谷歌避税引舆论关注

【知识点】

跨国公司、国际逃税、国际避税、国际税收管辖权

【案例介绍】

作为全球知名的跨国公司龙头企业之一，谷歌在全球诸多国家和地区都设有自己的管理机构和分公司。2017年7月，法国税务部门向巴黎法院指控谷歌利用税务漏洞，逃避了本应缴纳的11.2亿欧元税款。法国政府认为，谷歌从法国获得了巨额收入，但在法国仅缴纳了最低额的公司税。谷歌为了逃避缴纳法国公司税，将其在法国的收益转入了爱尔兰。但此案件的最终结果却是谷歌赢了这场官司。

英国《泰晤士报》曾在 2009 年报道，谷歌公司 2008 年从英国获得了 16 亿英镑的广告利润，但却并未缴纳税款。2009 年 11 月，土耳其的税务机关向谷歌开出了 7100 万土耳其里拉的罚单，并极力声讨谷歌的避税行为。

【案例分析】

本案例主要介绍了谷歌的国际避税事实和行为。作为拥有全球最大搜索引擎的科技巨头，谷歌公司每年拥有巨额收入，这也意味着谷歌要缴纳相应的税费。

根据美国税法规定，美国公司应缴纳其海外利润 25% ～ 35% 的税，而相关数据表明，谷歌每年缴税税率仅为 2.4%。一方面，谷歌利用避税地的存在来进行价格转移，从而使税负大幅降低。谷歌注册不同的离岸公司作为子公司，在税率高的地区集中支出，而将收入集中在税率极低的"避税天堂"百慕大。另一方面，因为无形资产具有非实体性、价值不可比性和收益不确定性等特殊性质，所以利用无形资产转让定价的方式进行避税更具隐蔽性，也不易被税务机构察觉。谷歌正是巧妙地利用了这一特性，通过出售知识产权的使用权，有效实现了避税。

谷歌采取的是"双层爱尔兰汉堡"和"荷兰三明治"模式，即"谷歌爱尔兰控股公司—荷兰—谷歌爱尔兰公司"模式。首先，谷歌爱尔兰控股公司是谷歌位于百慕大的一家具有控股性质的子公司，负责买进谷歌在美国开发的知识产权和在欧洲、非洲及中东地区的特许权，然后转让给谷歌爱尔兰公司，由于在转让过程中收取的是知识产权授权费，因此谷歌可以在爱尔兰巧妙地避税。谷歌爱尔兰公司是谷歌爱尔兰控股公司旗下的都柏林业务部，也是无形资产使用权的最终归属方，该公司主要向全球销售谷歌网络广告，创造的利润占公司海外总利润的 88%，该公司最终以支付知识产权使用费的形式把收入转移给百慕大的谷歌爱尔兰控股公司。因为谷歌并不属于欧盟成员国公司，不能享受爱尔兰地区的税收优惠，所以为避开在爱尔兰交税，谷歌爱尔兰公司便利用了荷兰无员工的空壳公司，先付款给荷兰空壳公司，再由荷兰空壳公司把约 99.8% 的特许权使用费转到百慕大。虽然过程较为复杂周折，但是却为谷歌提高了约 26% 的利润，节省了近 31 亿美元的税务开支。

虽然谷歌在法国避税案中获得了胜诉，但其避税行为依然引起一些国家的不满。此前，意大利税务部门指控谷歌在 2009—2013 年的总避税金额约 3.06 亿欧元，这些钱都被谷歌转移到了爱尔兰。随后，谷歌公司决定就税收争议与意大利达成和解，向意大利政府补缴拖欠的税款。2016 年，欧盟为打击跨国公司避税行为，推出了新的条例，要求年营业收入超过 7.5 亿欧元并且在欧盟范围内注册的大型跨国公司，必须每年向欧盟报告该公司当年在欧盟各成员国的营业收入，以及向其他国家纳税的情况。

【结论】

国际税收法律制度实践性较强，不仅涉及国际税法的主体和客体，而且还涉及国际税收基本关系。作为跨国纳税义务人，跨国公司必须遵守东道国相关税收制度的规定，否则将承担相应的法律后果。随着国际税收合作的开展，跨国公司的国际避税与国际逃税空间也将越来越小。

【案例来源】

何雨璠.浅析谷歌避税问题及对我国带来的启示[J]. 今日财富, 2017（24）：8-9.

【案例问题】

结合谷歌公司的避税案例，试理解打击国际逃税与国际避税的现实意义。

第**3**章

跨国直接投资

3.1　东方国际海外绿地投资

【知识点】

国际直接投资、绿地投资、投资环境、法律环境

【案例介绍】

2020 年 9 月 22 日，东方国际集团埃塞毛衫制造基地建设项目（一期）正式开工。该项目是东方国际集团响应"一带一路"倡议，践行"走出去"战略，在海外实施绿地投资的"第一单"，也是迄今为止最大的一单。

该项目位于埃塞俄比亚首都亚的斯亚贝巴国家工业园"二期"，项目（一期）共建设 3 幢毛衫生产车间，建设总投资额为 3 亿元人民币，总建筑面积为 6.2 万平方米，共配置 1200 台电脑横机、2000 台套口机。项目计划建设工期为一年，建成后可形成 1000 万件毛衫产能，是集团打造毛衫核心能力建设、开拓欧美市场、实现产能国际化的重要布局。虽然新冠肺炎疫情让全球经济按下暂停键，也让我国对外投资合作项目受到较大影响，但是这项看似在新冠肺炎疫情期间"不可能完成的任务"，东方国际集团埃塞项目团队却做到了。

【案例分析】

东方国际集团正一步一个脚印地稳步走好国际产能合作之路。作为上海最大的外贸企业，东方国际集团积极响应国家倡议，利用国际产能进行合作投资。

东方国际集团践行国际化战略，在全球范围安排生产制造、贸易销售、技术研发、供应链物流及广泛开展经贸投资合作，将工厂陆续布局在"一带一路"沿线国家，将"中国制造"转变为"海外制造"。在非洲，东方国际集团深度考察研究了

埃塞俄比亚、科特迪瓦和布基纳法索等国的情况，以期利用当地政策优势及劳动力、原料优势，把握国际产能合作和转移的经济规律，不断拓展集团在海外的"疆土"。

在全球面临新冠肺炎疫情的大背景下，东方国际集团采取了积极稳健的投资战略，从而保障了集团在非洲的投资建设项目得以顺利完成。为确保 2020 年 9 月 22 日项目正式开工，由 7 人组成的外派团队于 2020 年 8 月底埃塞俄比亚新冠肺炎疫情严重之时，毅然出征。经过百天奋战，该团队克服了集装箱荒、海运费及主材价格上涨等诸多困难，于 2020 年 12 月 31 日完成现场 3 个主车间所有基础施工及车间一的主钢结构安装（钢梁、钢柱、檩条、楼承板）和验收工作，国内后勤组也同步完成钢结构等各类物资（共 275 箱）的发运工作，及时满足了现场连续施工的要求。2021 年 2 月底，现场施工各分项质量验收均一次性通过，最终现场完成进度较计划工期提前近一个月。

东方国际集团积极推动国际文化交流。早在 2018 中非合作论坛北京峰会上，习近平总书记就特别提到对非洲青年人才的培养问题，尤其是要向非洲青年提供职业技能培训，提供更多就业机会、更好发展空间。东方国际集团积极响应，充分调动教育优势资源，发挥教育的基础性、先导性和保障性作用。近年来，东方国际在非洲建立多处教育培训基地，如 2018 年 9 月在埃塞俄比亚首都亚的斯亚贝巴市与东华大学共同创建"纺织'一带一路'教育培训基地（非洲）"。此外，东方国际所属的"东方时尚发展部"就上海时装周等项目与意大利联合会签订合作谅解备忘录，实行资源共享，优势互补，拓展了东方国际集团时尚产业发展的深度和广度。

由本案例可见，企业在进行国际投资之前应先从企业自身战略出发，分析东道国的投资环境，考虑企业是否可以在此次投资中提高自身竞争力，然后选择是否进行绿地投资。如果企业在经济发展程度低的地区以绿地投资模式进入，那么它所面临的门槛会比较低，而且在与当地企业的竞争中也会处于优势地位。但是，企业需要投入大量资金和时间建立新的营销网络，获得利益相关者的文化认同及一定的外部合法性。

【结论】

绿地投资的投资建设周期较长，需要企业进行长期的资金投入，因此投资风险较大，而且企业在投资初期会面临东道国的文化差异、政府管制、现有企业排挤、内部企业组织经营管理等方面的困难。东方国际集团在绿地投资方面的成功经验对于中国其他"走出去"的企业具有很好的借鉴意义。

【案例来源】

金琳. 东方国际海外绿地投资"第一单"［J］. 上海国资，2021（2）：61-62.

【案例问题】

（1）试评价东方国际集团海外投资的法律环境。

（2）在国际直接投资中，绿地投资一般会涉及东道国的哪些法律问题？

3.2 "三一重工"成功并购案

【知识点】

国际直接投资、跨国并购、文化整合

【案例介绍】

近年来，中国工程机械行业的市场逐渐饱和，该行业内的企业面临的压力与日俱增。相对而言，国外市场则具有巨大的开发潜力。"三一重工"在进行跨国并购前，国内市场是其关键市场，国际市场的销售收入仅占 10%。但开发国外市场后，"三一重工"的情况发生了较大变化。

对于德国普茨迈斯特而言，2008 年的金融危机对其经济效益造成了巨大打击。除此之外，作为家族式企业，创始人的子女并不想延续该行业的经营。以上两个因素构成了普茨迈斯特创始人急于出售该企业的原因。2011 年 12 月 20 日，普茨迈斯特访问

"三一重工"并向其发出竞购邀约。2012 年 1 月初，"三一重工"对普茨迈斯特发出信件，将合作的想法传达给对方，随后定下初步并购意向。2012 年 1 月 31 日，"三一重工"对外宣布，将联合中信产业投资基金出资 3.6 亿欧元收购普茨迈斯特 90% 股权。2013 年 7 月 1 日，"三一重工"收购普茨迈斯特剩余 10% 股权，实现 100% 控股。

【案例分析】

本案例主要介绍了中国工程机械行业的龙头企业"三一重工"对德国普茨迈斯特的并购，这次成功并购使双方企业都获得了较好的发展。

从生产成本方面来看，"三一重工"凭借并购在短期内获得了普茨迈斯特领先的技术支持，降低了创新风险，巩固了其在产业链中的地位，并缩减了成本。对普茨迈斯特而言，通过利用中国的劳动力成本优势，降低了生产总成本，从而进一步提升了自身的盈利能力。

从市场份额方面来看，普茨迈斯特拥有享誉全球的品牌，且在发达国家拥有较高的市场份额，工厂遍布世界，销售和服务站点更是遍及全球 100 多个国家和地区，但是其"高质量高定价"的营销模式在中国市场的发展却十分有限。对于普茨迈斯特来说，此次并购也有助于解决其在中国市场"水土不服"的问题，有助于节约生产成本，提升在中国市场的占有率。而对于"三一重工"来说，本次并购使其大幅提升了自己的市场占有率。

从国际化方面来看，普茨迈斯特良好的品牌形象帮助"三一重工"拓宽了国际化发展道路，加快了"三一重工"进入欧美市场的速度。不仅如此，"三一重工"还从普茨迈斯特学到了国际领先的管理理念与方法，提升了自身的国际化经营水准。

由于普茨迈斯特在德国机械领域独占鳌头，其企业文化相对成熟，品牌形象享誉世界，因此，只有确保了普茨迈斯特的品牌独立性，才能有效维护品牌价值，从而尽可能地提升并购整合成效。"三一重工"在并购后的文化整合中所采取的"先隔离后融合"式策略起到了非常重要的作用，该策略大幅降低了文化整合的成本和风险，尽可能地维护和保留了普茨迈斯特的自主性和独立性，"三一重工"在此基础之上逐步展开文化整合，使两家企业既能在一定程度上各自独立运作，又能相互学习、相互支援，最终达到双赢的目的。

【结论】

跨国并购是企业国际化的重要特征。跨国并购既要准确评估企业并购前后的生产成本、市场份额，又要重视企业的品牌价值。此外，企业国际化拓展中的文化因素、文化风险及文化整合也是需要企业高度重视的方面。

【案例来源】

王博文."蛇吞象"式跨国并购中的文化冲突与整合策略：以三一重工并购德国普茨迈斯特为例［J］.国际商务财会，2021（9）：42-46.

【案例问题】

（1）"三一重工"成功并购普茨迈斯特有哪些值得借鉴的经验？

（2）国际直接投资中的并购与绿地投资有何区别？

3.3 明基并购西门子的教训

【知识点】

国际直接投资、跨国并购、文化冲突、文化融合

【案例介绍】

明基早在2005年就已经成为世界第一大手机代工厂商，但明基一直希望能够拥有自主品牌，只是单靠明基的力量还无法实现。因此，并购一家与之相关的知名国际品牌就成了明基的首选。恰好，西门子和摩托罗拉之间的谈判失败给明基创造

了机会。2005 年 6 月 8 日，明基正式宣布并购西门子手机业务。当时，这被外界视为一笔非常划算的交易，因为明基分文未出，而西门子还另外补贴明基 2.5 亿欧元。但实际上，明基虽然获得了西门子在 GSM、GPRS、3G 领域的核心专利技术，但西门子手机每日的巨额亏损也给明基带来了沉重的负担。

【案例分析】

这是一起失败的中国企业并购国外企业的案例。尽管明基在收购前已经为接受西门子手机业务做好了充分的准备，但事后企业的整合特别是两家企业的文化调和却一直没有达到预期目标，具体原因分析如下。

（1）由于西门子的"慢"文化与明基的"快"文化存在着较大的差异，因此二者的整合难度较大。作为欧洲知名的大型企业，西门子的企业文化也非常有名。而明基作为一个中国新兴的企业，很难吸收甚至改变西门子的文化。在战略上，西门子追求高质量、高品质的产品，关注创新，而以代工出身的明基则更关注产品的设计和顾客的需求。在管理上，明基是一个创业型组织，强调创新和速度，而西门子则是一个管理型组织，更强调规范和程序。在运营管理上，西门子强调程序和规章的完整性，明基则更具灵活性。这样两种截然不同的企业文化碰撞在了一起，一个是快速、弹性、机会型，一个是稳健、规范、完美型，双方无论是企业体系还是社会体系都相差太远。

（2）对于目标企业的文化研究不够。在签订并购协议之前，企业应通过组建调查团队，采用合理、系统和科学的方法，对并购目标的国家文化、企业历史和发展战略等深层次问题进行调查与分析，然后与自身的企业文化及整合后的企业文化进行匹配。如果双方的文化差异性很大，以至于整合的可能性很小，那么企业就应该果断地放弃这次并购。

（3）明基在整合过程还受到德国政治、文化和法律等方面的一些影响。这种直接的文化与体制冲突风险加大了整合成本，如德国对本地劳工强有力的保护体系和当地各种组织力量的干扰，导致明基无法降低德国员工的薪酬水平，并且囿于当地法律的限制，明基也无法裁员减负。

（4）企业战略与文化协调不足。企业战略与文化的协调是一个动态的过程，在这一过程中，一定要让员工切身感受和认同这些变化，切忌单纯为了企业文化而整合，因为这样不但会增加整合的成本，还可能导致双方互不认同。在企业发展中，文化实际上是不可比较的，即没有所谓的优劣之分，只有适合还是不适合企业的战略发展。如果企业文化能与企业战略融为一体，那么就能够推动企业可持续发展。

【结论】

明基并购西门子，是中国企业跨国并购中一个令人惋惜的因企业文化冲突而失败的案例。总结失败的原因，可以得出如下结论：企业并购前应做好综合衡量与准备，做好被并购方及其所在国家的文化评估；并购后对目标企业要做好战略整合与文化融合的有机统一。

【案例来源】

余典范.中国企业海外并购文化整合失败的案例与经验教训.企业文明［J］.2013（9）：27-29.

【案例问题】

结合国际直接投资的有关内容，试总结明基并购西门子失败的主要教训。

3.4 "一带一路"与国际投资

【知识点】

国际直接投资、跨国并购、股权转让与法律规制

【案例介绍】

以色列以其高产奶牛和先进的乳业生产技术而闻名。Tnuva 是以色列最大的综合食品企业之一，已有 80 多年的历史。Tnuva 的乳制品在以色列市场所占的份额超过 50%，其在乳品研发制造、牧业养殖及管理等方面都处于世界领先水平。英国私募股权投资公司 Apax Partner 持有 Tnuva 56.7% 的股份，以色列投资公司 Mivtach Shamir 持有 21% 的股份，其余股份则由当地集体社区和农业合作社持有。

光明食品于 2013 年 9 月开始接触 Tnuva，此时 Tnuva 的大股东 Apax Partner 正在筹备 Tnuva 上市，但在了解了光明食品的相关信息之后，Apax Partner 决定中止上市进程并与光明食品展开谈判合作。拥有随售权的股东 Mivtach Shamir 公司表示，将保留股权并与光明食品合作。2014 年 5 月 22 日，光明食品与 Apax Partner 就收购 Tnuva 股权事宜达成初步收购协议。

2014 年 8 月，光明食品收购 Tnuva 56% 股权的申请获得了商务部批准。此次海外并购由光明食品与国内一家金融机构共同出资，二者分别持有 36% 和 20% 的股权。2015 年 1 月是原定的交割时间，但在交割前夕，小股东 Mivtach Shamir 突然提出要使用随售权，跟随大股东出售其股权。如想要其保留股权，光明食品就要接受其他商业条件。如果不能按时交割，光明食品就要付出高昂的违约金。此时，光明食品有两种选择，要么单独增资购买，但需要再次审批（商务部审批一般需要 3 个月左右）；要么寻找合作伙伴，或要求原合作伙伴增资。但原来共同出资的合作机构因为交易前景无法预测，决定退出，不再参与此次收购。

在光明食品的一再要求下，Apax Partner 最后同意将交割期从 2015 年 1 月延迟至 2015 年 4 月，条件是光明食品将违约金打进一个公管账号，如果 3 个月后不能完成交割，违约金将归 Apax Partner 所有。最终光明食品在规定日期里完成了审批，并按时进行了交割，表现出了极强的应变能力。

2015 年 6 月 8 日，光明乳业发布公告，称公司拟向信晟投资、晟创投资、益民集团、上汽投资、国盛投资和浦科源富达壹 6 家机构定向增发，预计募集资金 90 亿元，发行价格为 16.1 元 / 股，发行数量不超过 5.59 亿股。其中 68.73 亿元用于收购母公司持有的光明食品新加坡投资有限公司 100% 股权，从而获得其所持有的 Tnuva 76.7% 的控制权，剩余募集资金则用于补充流动资金。8 月 10 日，上海国资委批准光明乳业最多可通过非公开发行筹集 90 亿元人民币。同年 8 月 14 日，光明乳业召开 2015 年第一次临时股东大会，通过了非公开发行 A 股股票等议案。但是，2016 年 2 月 28 日，光明乳业却宣告终止非公开发行 A 股股票，原因是当时光明乳业的股票价格（10.76 元 / 股）远低于计划的发行价格（16.1 元 / 股），基本无法获得机构认购。同年 3 月 17 日，光明乳业发布公告，与大股东光明食品旗下子公司光明食品国际及光明食品新加坡投资有限公司重新签订托管协议，将 Tnuva 76.7% 的股权交由光明乳业托管。

【案例分析】

本案例主要介绍了光明食品成功收购以色列 Tnuva 的过程。从战略安排上讲，这是继光明食品并购新西兰新莱特公司后，企业国际化的又一个亮点。

以色列虽然耕地贫瘠、水源奇缺，但农业发展水平相当高。其中养牛技术更是世界领先，良种奶牛单产可达 12 吨，位居全球第一，养牛业产值占农业总产值的 14%。而近年来，我国进口奶量每年都以较高的增速在增长。通过此次并购，Tnuva 的优质产品，包括有机酸奶、奶酪、鲜奶、黄油、甜点、乳清粉等，可以借助光明食品在中国的渠道优势进入中国市场，进而推动 Tnuva 的全球化发展。

对光明食品来说，其旗下新莱特生产的奶粉可以满足以色列产奶淡季的奶源供应，形成以色列、新西兰、中国三地业务互动，从而产生较强的协同效应。另外，Tnuva 不仅是以色列最大的乳制品企业，其在肉类、冷冻食品等领域也具有优势。与 Tnuva 在技术研发、市场营销、渠道等方面形成协同效应，可以有效促进光明食品全产业链的精细化发展。

【结论】

光明食品并购以色列 Tnuva 是一个成功的国际直接投资案例。该案例为"一带一路"背景下中国企业国际化提供了一个可借鉴的样本，即企业在并购前与大股东进行前期接触，在并购后与被并购方在国际市场开拓、产品技术研发及原材料供给等多方面进行深入合作，从而实现协同效应。这同时说明，"一带一路"倡议的推进，加强了中国与沿线国家的合作，改变了中国企业海外并购的整体格局。

【案例来源】

张文佳."一带一路"背景下光明食品跨国并购案例分析[J].经济论坛，2018（4）：129–131.

【案例问题】

（1）光明食品跨国并购案有哪些启示？

（2）在"一带一路"背景下，中国企业在进行对外投资时可能会面临哪些法律风险？

3.5 国际投资争端与仲裁程序适用

【知识点】

国际投资、《关于解决国家与他国国民间投资争端公约》（又称《华盛顿公约》）、国际投资争端解决机制、管辖权

【案例介绍】

塞佩姆（Saipem）为一家在意大利注册的公司，主要从事石油和天然气管道铺设业务。1990 年 2 月 14 日，Saipem 和孟加拉国一家名为孟加拉国石油的国有企业签订合同，在孟加拉国铺设石油和天然气管道，管道长度为 409 千米，合同造价约

3400 万美元。该项目由世界银行及其下属的国际开发协会提供贷款。合同规定项目应于 1991 年 4 月 30 日完成，但由于在铺设管道的过程中，该项目遇到当地居民反对以及一些其他问题，合同双方同意将完工时间推迟一年。由于孟加拉国石油没有按合同规定向 Saipem 支付预付款，且双方无法就 Saipem 在工程延迟过程中的额外开支达成协议，Saipem 于 1993 年 6 月 7 日根据双方的合同向国际商会仲裁院提起仲裁。

仲裁庭组成后，孟加拉国石油向孟加拉国法院提起诉讼，认为依据孟加拉国法律，该争议不能以仲裁解决。1997 年 11 月 24 日，孟加拉国最高法院发布禁止令，责令 Saipem 停止在国际商会仲裁院的仲裁。2000 年 4 月 5 日，达卡初级法院否决了国际商会仲裁院的裁决权。2001 年 4 月 30 日，国际商会仲裁院决定继续仲裁，并于 2003 年 5 月 9 日裁定孟加拉国石油败诉，判其偿付 Saipem 600 余万美元及 11 万欧元。

在国际商会仲裁庭做出裁决后，孟加拉国石油向当地法院起诉，要求撤销国际商会仲裁院的裁决。2004 年 4 月 21 日，孟加拉国最高法院驳回了孟加拉国石油的申请，指出根据孟加拉国的法律，国际商会仲裁院的裁决自始无效，因此也就没有撤销的问题。2004 年 10 月 5 日，Saipem 依据孟加拉国和意大利之间签订的双边投资保护协定向国际投资争端解决中心提起仲裁。

【案例分析】

本案例主要介绍了 Saipem 和孟加拉国石油的合同项目（在孟加拉国铺设石油和天然气管道）所产生的争议，以及争议的解决途径和司法管辖权问题。分析该案例，需要从以下几方面入手。

（1）Saipem 可否向国际商会仲裁院提起仲裁？

（2）孟加拉国法院可否否决国际商会仲裁院的裁决？

（3）此案是否可以援引《华盛顿公约》有关规定？

（4）此案例争议是否适用国际投资争端解决中心的仲裁程序？

一般来说，国际商事争议可以提请国际商会仲裁院等机构仲裁，但首先争议当事人必须是一致同意的。如果 Saipem 和孟加拉国石油在订立合同时写明了争议发生时适用孟加拉国国内法，那么，一方单独提请仲裁是不恰当的。在本案例中，一方提请仲裁，一方寻求国内法保护，导致问题难以解决。在此情况下，如果双方的母国都是《华盛顿公约》的缔约方，则可以考虑争议是否属于《华盛顿公约》第 25 条下的投资，以及相关争议是否直接源自投资。结合本案例详情，Saipem 依据孟加拉国和意大利之间签订的双边投资保护协定，向国际投资争端解决中心提起仲裁是正确的。

【结论】

此案可以援引《华盛顿公约》有关规定，案例争议适用国际投资争端解决中心仲裁程序。同时，孟加拉国和意大利之间签订的双边投资保护协定也是解决案例争议的依据。

【案例来源】

张海燕，邓婷婷 . 国际经济法典型案例评析 [M]. 长沙：中南大学出版社，2016.

【案例问题】

《华盛顿公约》及其争端解决机制与程序是什么？

3.6　最惠国待遇原则的适用

【知识点】

国际投资、投资协定、投资保护、最惠国待遇

【案例介绍】

阿根廷投资者马菲兹尼（Maffezini）在西班牙投资建立了一个化工厂，后与当地政府产生争议。根据西班牙与阿根廷 1991 年双边投资保护协定第 10 条的规定，在向国际投资争端解决中心提起仲裁之前，Maffezini 必须先向西班牙法院寻求司法救济。然而，西班牙与智利 1991 年签订的双边投资协定第 10 条却只要求先进行磋商，然后缔约一方投资者就可以将缔约另一方政府诉诸国际投资争端解决中心。因西班牙与阿根廷之间双边投资保护协定第 4 条规定，"本协定项下的所有事项都可适用最惠国待遇原则"。据此，Maffezini 要求获得西班牙与智利双边投资协定第 10 条规定的待遇，即无须向西班牙法院起诉就可直接向国际投资争端解决中心提起仲裁。

【案例分析】

本案例介绍了阿根廷投资者在西班牙投资时与当地政府产生的争议。争议主要涉及最惠国待遇原则和投资协定的适用问题。

1. 最惠国待遇的适用问题

最惠国待遇，是指东道国按本国法律给予外国投资者的待遇，不低于或不少于该国给予任何第三国投资者的待遇。即缔约一方投资者在缔约另一方境内的投资所享受的待遇，不应低于同缔约另一方订有同类协定的第三国投资者的投资所享有的待遇。同时，缔约一方投资者在缔约另一方境内进行与投资有关活动所享受的待遇，不应低于同缔约另一方订有同类协定的第三国投资者进行与投资有关的活动所享有的待遇。其中与投资有关的"活动"是指"一项投资的管理、维护、使用、享有和处分"。

在以往的案例中最惠国待遇条款适用的范围是"事项"。"事项"是指实体方面的事项，并不包括管辖权及其他程序事项，因此并不符合"同类原则"。但是考虑到当今的争端解决安排与投资者保护之间有强烈的关联性，如果针对第三国投资者的争端条款中对外国投资者利益的保护比基础条约中的当地救济条款更有利，那么，最惠国待遇原则就适用于程序事项。

2. 双边投资协定的适用问题

一般来说，国际投资协定的缔约者为了保护本国投资者的利益，都会在协定中规定投资者所享有的待遇。依据西班牙与阿根廷之间双边投资保护协定第 4 条的规定，该协定项下的所有事项都可适用最惠国待遇原则。由此可见，双边投资保护协定是享有最惠国待遇的直接依据。

【结论】

阿根廷投资者 Maffezini 要求获得与西班牙和智利双边投资协定第 10 条规定同样的待遇，以及未向西班牙法院起诉就直接向国际投资争端解决中心提起仲裁的做法是合理的。案例中的最惠国待遇适用于程序事项。

【案例来源】

王海英. 国际经济法案例教程［M］. 2 版. 北京：北京大学出版社，2012.

【案例问题】

双边投资协定中的最惠国待遇条款是否适用于程序事项？

3.7　华为遭遇美国歧视性待遇

【知识点】

国际投资、市场准入、歧视性待遇

【案例介绍】

2019 年 5 月，美国首次制裁华为，要求华为不能使用美国产的电子设计自动化技术（Electronic Design Automation，EDA）和谷歌地图，但是华为可以继续使用已经采购的 EDA 进行芯片设计。

2020 年 5 月 15 日，美国对华为的制裁升级，开始针对华为芯片业务。使用 EDA 技术的厂家，如台积电、中芯国际等也不能再为华为生产芯片。不过，华为还是可以委托第三方生产芯片，或者直接从联发科技（MTK）或者三星这些不受美国管控的公司订购芯片。2020 年 8 月 17 日，美国修改了制裁条件，规定联发科技和三星这些基于美国技术进行软件生产的公司也不得为华为生产芯片。此外，美国还增加了对华为子公司云服务业务的制裁。

美国还限制华为收购；禁止华为进入美国市场；以安全为理由游说和威胁他国，使其拒绝华为 5G 技术；对麒麟芯片进行技术封锁。此外，鸿蒙操作系统、华为移动服务、华为软件商店等也遭到了美国的全方位围追堵截。

【案例分析】

本案例介绍了美国对华为公司的一系列限制和制裁措施，主要涉及阻断各国对华为技术的使用和芯片厂商对华为的芯片供应。

美国在 2017 年就已开始对中兴和华为采取制裁措施。2017 年 3 月 22 日，美国司法部以中兴违反《伊朗制裁禁令》，向伊朗出口美国管制的产品为由，对中兴提起诉讼。这就导致中芯国际不能给华为提供芯片，从而扼制了华为的发展。美国对华为制裁中所涉及的"实体清单"和"制裁禁令"是美国实施经济制裁时常用的手段。这些制裁的运行是以美国的域外管辖为基础的。

随着技术在国际上的地位越来越重要，美国对华为的制裁也一步步升级。美国不仅限制华为收购，禁止华为进入美国市场，对华为进行技术封锁等，还通过一系列"泛安全化"的调查与司法指控给华为贴上"危害国家安全"的标签，并大肆进行关于华为的负面宣传，从而向美国企业和消费者施压，使其与华为保持商业距离。

美国在进行对外经济制裁时常常采用"美国优先"的政策理念，并且会在初级制裁的基础上通过次级制裁将制约范围扩大至第三国自然人或实体，将单边制裁体系扩大为多边制裁体系。

美国先后对中兴和华为采取制裁措施，随后又将多家中国实体列入"实体清单"，美国这样做的根本原因在于美国坚持"本国利益至上"，并意图维护其世界霸主地位。美国屡次通过其国内法案和行政命令单边制裁外国实体的行为实质上是美国国内法的域外适用，这种适用在国际法领域中是存在合法性争议的。

【结论】

随着全球经济一体化的发展和全球竞争的日益激烈，各国在国际事务中的摩擦和冲突进一步升级。同时，单边主义和逆全球化浪潮进一步加剧了各国通过制裁手段构建贸易壁垒和技术门槛的态势。在此背景下，中国及中国企业可从经济、法律和发展策略等方面出发，运用清单体系、主权平等和阻断立法等措施予以反制。

【案例来源】

［1］孟刚，王晔琼.美国一级制裁的理论基础与制度实践［J］.中财法律评论，2020，12（0）：75-92.

［2］霍达.国际反制裁制度体系的构建与启示［J］.人民论坛，2021（31）：88-92.

［3］于方容，王敏.当前美国经济制裁的法律分析及中方对策：以华为、中兴为例［J］.现代商贸工业，2021，42（33）：26-28.

【案例问题】

如何评价华为公司在美国遭遇的歧视性待遇？

3.8　外国投资者的待遇标准

【知识点】

国际投资、公平与公正待遇、分成合同

【案例介绍】

1999 年 5 月 21 日，厄瓜多尔政府通过厄瓜多尔国家石油公司与西方石油公司的全资子公司西方石油勘探和生产公司签订"分成合同"，共同开发厄瓜多尔境内的第 15 号石油区块油田。"分成合同"规定，转让该合同项下第 22 款的权利或义务须经厄瓜多尔当局批准。此后，因西方石油勘探和生产公司将"分成合同"项下的 40% 权益转让给注册于百慕大的 A 公司（A 公司随后转售给中国某公司），厄瓜多尔能源与矿业部颁发"失效法令"，单方终止了"分成合同"。

2006 年 7 月，西方石油勘探和生产公司申请仲裁程序，在仲裁程序中，争议主要包括仲裁庭是否有管辖权，西方石油勘探和生产公司未经厄瓜多尔政府批准的转让行为是否发生效力，西方石油勘探和生产公司的转让行为是否必然导致"分成合同"的终止，厄瓜多尔政府单方终止"分成合同"是否违反美国、厄瓜多尔双边投资协定项下的公平与公正待遇和征收条款等。

仲裁庭认为，"分成合同"本身及厄瓜多尔法律均规定，转让"分成合同"的权利义务须经厄瓜多尔当局批准，因此，西方石油勘探和生产公司未经批准而擅自转让合同的行为确有不当。但是，转让行为未经批准这一事实并不导致"分成合同"终止，以终止合同来惩罚西方石油勘探和生产公司不符合公平原则。

2012 年 10 月，厄瓜多尔申请撤销程序。2015 年 11 月 2 日，国际投资争端解决中心专门委员会以"明显超越权限"为由，部分撤销"西方石油勘探和生产公司诉厄瓜多尔政府案"的仲裁裁决。经审理，专门委员会认为原案申请人西方石油勘探和生产公司仅对该案合同标的"第 15 号石油区块油田"享有 60% 的权益，遂将其对厄瓜多尔的赔偿金额降至原赔偿额的 60%，即 10.6 亿美元。原裁决其余内容的效力不受部分撤销的影响。

【案例分析】

本案例介绍了厄瓜多尔与西方石油勘探和生产公司因"分成合同"而引起的争议及其仲裁结果。本案例涉及国际投资的相关条款。

（1）公平与公正待遇条款。在国际投资争议仲裁中，公平与公正待遇条款经常被援引和适用。除个别案例外，国际投资争端解决中心仲裁的大部分案件都涉及公平与公正待遇条款，因此该条款被誉为国际投资法领域的帝王条款。

（2）公平与公正待遇条款的适用。在国际投资仲裁实践中，认为可以归入违反公平与公正待遇条款的情形达 11 种，主要包括违反正当程序、实行专断的和歧视性措施、损害外国投资者的合法期待及缺乏透明度等。

随着国际投资的不断发展、国际投资形式和种类的不断创新，新的投资争议类型不断涌现，有关公平与公正待遇也会出现不同的新情况。

【结论】

只有将公平与公正待遇严格限定在经国际习惯法之构成要件检验的范围内，即东道国不违反正当程序，不采取歧视性行为和不实行专断措施等，才能使公平与公正待遇符合双边投资协定的宗旨，限制关于公平与公正待遇方面的"法官造法"，保证双边投资条约"国家造法"的性质。

【案例来源】

张海燕，邓婷婷.国际经济法典型案例评析[M].长沙：中南大学出版社，2016.

【案例问题】

（1）公平与公正待遇原则一般应该包含哪些内容？

（2）公平与公正待遇原则的适用是否应当受到限制？

第4章

国际商事合同

4.1 销售合同与反倾销税

【知识点】

货物进出口、销售合同、FOB、反倾销税

【案例介绍】

买方（美国某进口商）与卖方（中国某出口商）于 2015—2016 年签订 5 份某商品的销售合同。在双方履行合同后，因交易涉及美国反倾销税问题而产生争议。买方主张，由于卖方过错（提供了错误的进口商名称）且卖方未能积极配合买方为其提供相关证明文件而导致买方在货物目的地美国缴纳反倾销税，因此要求卖方承担反倾销税。而卖方主张，由于合同约定的交货条件是中国某港口船上交货（Free On Board，FOB），在 FOB 条件下，缴纳进口关税的责任在买方，因此买方应自行承担反倾销税。

【案例分析】

本案例的主要争议是买卖双方因销售合同引出的反倾销税的承担问题。

下面将以仲裁庭的认定结果为依据进行分析。

仲裁庭认为，反倾销税是针对该案卖方销售的货物价格低于成本价或者出口国当地市场价格，影响进口国同类货物的经营者的业务而发起的征税行为，该税的征收对象是美国的进口方，征税的时间是在货物进入美国海关的当时或之后。因此，在 FOB 条件下缴纳税费的义务应由买方承担。

但由于卖方错误地提供了进口商的名称，而且卖方未能积极配合买方为其提供相关证明文件，因此卖方也有一定的责任，即卖方违反了合同的通知和协助义务。因此，卖方应当对此损失负有部分责任。仲裁庭最终裁定，卖方对买方反倾销税损失承担 50% 的责任。

【结论】

买卖双方应为对方履行义务提供必要协助的义务，不仅源于《国际贸易术语解释通则》中的规定，也源于交易合同中对诚实信用原则的规定。

【案例来源】

中国国际经济贸易仲裁委员会. 中国国际商事仲裁年度报告（2019—2020）［M］.北京：法律出版社，2020.

【案例问题】

试比较《国际贸易术语解释通则 2010》与《国际贸易术语解释通则 2020》的异同。

4.2 鱼粉进口合同引索赔

【知识点】

国际贸易、国际货物买卖合同、CFR 风险转移

【案例介绍】

2000 年 3 月 6 日，原告青岛某公司作为买方与被告美国某公司以 "506.5 美元 /吨成本加运费（Cost and Freight，CFR）青岛" 的贸易条件订立了一份进口 5000 吨智利鱼粉的合同。合同规定的质量要求为：卖方所交鱼粉在装船港应不含有任何活昆虫、沙门氏菌和志贺氏菌。

交货期限：2000年4月至5月交3000吨，5月至6月交2000吨。

付款条件：买方应于2000年3月15日以前向中国银行青岛分行申请开立以卖方为受益人的不可撤销的即期信用证。信用证有效期为提单日期后35天，卖方须于6月30日以前在香港交单。此外，合同还规定由买方按伦敦协会条款投保一切险。议付单据包括由第三方检测、鉴定机构出具的全套装船检验单证，买方保留在目的港的复检权。

卖方于5月31日将3150吨鱼粉装"征服"轮，并于6月30日在香港提交了全套议付单据，但因单据中有个字母打错而遭拒付。7月22日，"征服"轮抵达青岛港卸货；7月31日，买方电告卖方："鱼粉发现大量拟白腹皮蠹活虫"；8月2日，鱼粉卸毕进仓；8月3日，买方传真要求卖方提供保险单，遭婉拒后以鱼粉生虫为由扣付20%货款，并向卖方索赔105万美元。

【案例分析】

本案例涉及国际贸易项下的货物进出口买卖合同，合同的主体、合同标的物数量和标准、合同价格、支付方式、交货条款约定等都比较清晰。合同产生争议的问题单一、明确，即货物质量存在瑕疵。

CFR贸易术语对买卖双方的权利和义务的主要规定是：买卖双方都没有强制性保险义务；货物于装运港装至船舶上之后的风险应当由买方承担；卖方必须就货物的交货给予买方充分的通知。

本案例中的标的物属于风险责任而非品质责任。卖方在装运港将货物装船即已完成交货义务，同时取得了全套装船检验单证，说明货物符合质量要求。

如果买方按照合同约定投保了伦敦协会条款的一切险，则无论鱼粉是由于外因还是其固有瑕疵生虫，都可以向保险人索赔。

【结论】

国际货物买卖合同中的贸易术语选择，决定了买卖双方的权利和义务。案例中的买方索赔事由不能成立。

【案例来源】

王海英.国际经济法案例教程［ M ］.2 版.北京：北京大学出版社，2012.

【案例问题】

在国际货物买卖中关于风险转移具体有哪些规定？

4.3　设备销售与安装合同纠纷

【知识点】

要约、承诺、《联合国国际货物销售合同公约》

【案例介绍】

原告：EAS 是一家主要从事自动化设备的设计、制造、整合及安装的公司，主要营业地位于美国密歇根州麦迪逊海茨市。

被告：TF 是一家位于加拿大新斯科舍省的公司，总部设在加拿大安大略省，主要为顾客提供重金属冲压件等设备。

EAS 与 TF 达成一项协议，约定由 EAS 为 TF 设计、制造及安装 Sport Bar 装备系统。2005 年 7 月 19 日，EAS 向 TF 发出了一系列报价，报价中载明为 TF 设计、制造 Sport Bar 装备系统设备，货物总价款为 540000 美元，交货日期是 2006 年 3 月 30 日；当天，TF 便口头上指示 EAS 可以开始着手 Sport Bar 装备系统的相关工作了。

2005 年 8 月 30 日，TF 签发了一份书面的订购单，其中包含一条法律适用条款：买家对卖家发出的要约做出承诺时，合同成立，合同成立的各方面内容必须适用买家总部注册地的法律，并按照该地的法律进行解释。任何关于合同的法律诉讼行为都必须在买家总部注册地所在省的法院提起，也就是说该合同引起的争议适用加拿大的法律。

2005年8月至10月，在EAS设计与制造Sport Bar装备系统设备期间，TF的代表就设备相关问题与EAS定期召开会议。2005年10月21日，TF的负责人指示EAS于2005年12月31日前交付Sport Bar装备系统设备，并完成位于加拿大安大略省Sport Bar装备系统的后续安装工作。

2005年12月31日，EAS将设备装船运往加拿大。EAS表明自己同意提前交付设备的原因是TF承诺会为加快安装Sport Bar装备系统做一些辅助工作，但实际上TF并没有兑现这些承诺。然而此时，EAS的员工已经在设施所在地安大略省为Sport Bar装备系统的安装、测试进行了相应的工作。之后，TF在继续运营着Sport Bar装备系统的同时，并没有付清剩余价款及相应利息。因此EAS对设备行使了"留置权"，并向美国地方法院提起诉讼，要求TF支付货物剩余价款及相应利息。而TF却主张合同中约定了争议适用加拿大的法律，因此要求美国地方法院以"不方便法院"为由驳回EAS的诉求。美国法院认为在最终确定适用的法律之前应驳回TF的请求。

【案例分析】

上述案例主要介绍了美国EAS公司和加拿大TF公司因设备销售、安装及费用给付产生的合同争议。

本案首先要解决的是法律的适用问题。2005年7月19日，EAS向TF发出了一系列报价，报价中载明了合同货物总价款和交货日期等信息。当天，TF口头上指示EAS可以开始着手Sport Bar装备系统的相关工作。这些法律事实表明，EAS的报价构成要约，TF口头上的同意行为构成承诺。

2005年8月30日，TF签发了一份书面的订购单，其中包含法律适用条款"买家对卖家发出的要约做出承诺时，合同成立"。这说明EAS和TF之间形成了国际货物销售合同关系，那么本案中由货物销售合同所引起的争议应适用《联合国国际货物销售合同公约》。

关于当事人 EAS 对设备行使"留置权"的问题，在《联合国国际货物销售合同公约》中没有相关规定，应根据国际私法规则确定的准据法加以判断。在本案中，EAS 的要约构成合同的主要内容，而合同的订立地、主要履行地都位于美国密歇根州，因此，商品留置权问题适用美国的专用工具留置权法，即原告 EAS 在被告 TF 支付剩余价款及相应的利息之前，有权留置该设备。

【结论】

美国 EAS 公司和加拿大 TF 公司所订立的合同成立，合同争议属于《联合国国际货物销售合同公约》调整范围。当事人 TF 履行合同付款义务后，当事人 EAS 可解除对设备行使的"留置权"。

【案例来源】

张海燕，邓婷婷.国际经济法典型案例评析［M］.长沙：中南大学出版社，2016.

【案例问题】

（1）依据《联合国国际货物销售合同公约》的规定，当一方违约时，另一方应当采取哪些补救措施？

（2）《联合国国际货物销售合同公约》对要约和承诺有哪些具体规定？

4.4　叉车出口合同涉风险转移

【知识点】

国际贸易、国际货物买卖合同、FOB、风险划分

【案例介绍】

2019 年，韩国 K 公司与马来西亚 M 公司签订了出口叉车的合同，贸易术语采用了船上交货（FOB），釜山港。2019 年 4 月 1 日，货物在装运时发生了意外，其中一辆叉车在吊装过程中不慎掉落在运船的甲板上而造成了损坏。所有货物于 4 月 2 日在装运港装船完毕。船长签发了已装船提单，提单说明：除了一辆叉车在装船过程中出现损坏，其余货物均表面良好。韩国 K 公司也于当日向马来西亚 M 公司发出了装船通知。货物于 4 月 15 日到达马来西亚。马来西亚 M 公司在提货时发现，除了提单上显示的叉车破损，其他车辆的表面也因货舱碰撞出现了划痕、变形、灯碎等多种破损情况。马来西亚 M 公司随后向韩国 K 公司提出索赔要求，理由是韩国 K 公司没有正确交付货物。韩国 K 公司则认为，根据合同，货物在装运港越过船舷后，其风险就已经发生转移，而货物的损失实际上发生在装运港越过船舷后，因此马来西亚 M 公司应自行承担损失。

【案例分析】

本案例涉及对国际货物买卖合同标的物的风险责任划分问题。

根据 FOB 贸易术语对买卖双方的权利和义务的主要规定，卖方必须在合同规定的日期或期间内在指定装运港将货物交至买方指定的船上，并承担货物安全交至船甲板上之前的一切费用和货物灭失或损坏的风险，货装船后买方须承担货物的全部费用、风险、灭失或损坏。FOB 明确指出它的风险划分界线是"装运港船上"，这说明卖方在装运港将货物交到买方所派船只的"船上"时，货物损坏或灭失的风险就由卖方转移至买方，也就是说从"完成装货"这一点来看，买家应承担货物损坏或毁灭的一切风险和费用。

在实际业务中，卖方必须向买方提供"已装船提单"，并发出"装货通知"，这表明按双方约定已由卖方承担货物装入船舱之前的一切风险和费用责任。另外，买卖双方都没有强制性保险义务，保险可由买方自愿购买。

【结论】

本案例中的卖方在装船完毕后签发了"已装船提单"和"装船通知"，而案例中的叉车是由于在货舱内发生相互碰撞而出现多处损坏的，发生的时间是在"装船"之后，这说明之前卖家已经完成了交货义务。因此，应由马来西亚 M 公司承担装船后的一切风险和费用。

【案例来源】

王海英. 国际经济法案例教程 [M]. 2 版 . 北京：北京大学出版社，2012.

【案例问题】

（1）国际货物买卖合同中的 FOB 术语是如何应用的？

（2）在 FOB 术语条件下，关于货物风险的转移及其责任条款有哪些具体规定？

4.5 "根本违反合同"条款

【知识点】

国际货物买卖合同、根本性违约、可预见性、延迟履行

【案例介绍】

买方（德国某公司）从卖方（意大利某公司）处订购了秋季款式的时装。合同规定卖方应当以分批的形式在 6 月至 9 月这一时间段内进行供货。但卖方的首批供货就已延迟，最后一批供货更是拖延到了 11 月 10 日。买方因此拒绝提货（也针对之前延迟的供货）。对此，协商无果后，买方将卖方诉讼至法院。

【案例分析】

这是一起买卖双方因延迟交付货物而产生的诉讼纠纷。合同当事人一方属于德国（买方），另一方属于意大利（卖方），因此合同争议属于《联合国国际货物销售合同公约》调整范畴。

按照《联合国国际货物销售合同公约》的规定，如果合同卖方发生了延迟供货，那么买方是否可以拒绝提货就取决于合同约定的供货时间，因为这里的时间约定具有法律意义。

在定期交易或季节性商品交易中，延迟供货本身就意味着根本性违约。买方是为了秋季的销售才购进该批秋季款式的时装的，而对于这一点卖方也很清楚。因此，卖方应当预见到，如果买方"直到秋季将尽时才能得到货物"，那么买方将很可能放弃合同。

【结论】

依据《联合国国际货物销售合同公约》第 25 条，可以认定卖方根本性违反合同的事实是存在的，因此，合同的买方有权拒绝提货并解除合同。

【案例来源】

施莱希特里姆.《联合国国际货物销售合同公约》评释：第 3 版[M].李慧妮，译.北京：北京大学出版社，2006.

【案例问题】

如何理解《联合国国际货物销售合同公约》中的"根本违反合同"条款及其适用条件？

4.6 "提货义务" 规则

【知识点】

《联合国国际货物销售合同公约》、实际履行、提取货物义务

【案例介绍】

一个意大利机器制造商（卖方）向一家法国公司（买方）出售印刷机。按照合同约定，卖方提供了货物，但买方在约定的提货时间内没有提取货物，其后对警告和给予的额外履行时间都没有回应。卖方最终宣布解除合同并要求买方赔偿损失。买方在辩护中声称，没有提货是因为放置机器的厂房没能及时建成，而卖方解除合同违反了诚信原则。

【案例分析】

本案例介绍了买卖双方订立合同后，在货物交付与提取货物环节所产生的争议。该争议属于《联合国国际货物销售合同公约》管辖范围。

一般来说，违反提取货物的义务并不能导致根本性违反合同。但这里有一些例外情形，如卖方必须准时清空他的仓库或者装载货物的运输工具，尤其是在出售大批量货物的情况下，因为卖方正常的生产经营要依赖于买方准时提取货物。

如果卖方已给予买方额外履行合同的时间，那么就说明卖方已经履行了合同义务，并实施了合同补救措施。在本案例中，卖方已经给予买方额外履行提取货物的时间，买方没有回应并拒绝提货，这就违反了提取货物的义务。

【结论】

按照《联合国国际货物销售合同公约》有关实际履行合同请求权和提取货物义务的条款，卖方的诉讼请求应当予以支持。

【案例来源】

施莱希特里姆.《联合国国际货物销售合同公约》评释：第 3 版［M］.李慧妮，译.北京：北京大学出版社，2006.

【案例问题】

如何理解《联合国国际货物销售合同公约》有关"提货义务"的规定？

第5章

国际货物运输

5.1 提单的运用

【知识点】

国际货物运输、托运人、承运人、提单

【案例介绍】

A 公司与 B 公司于 2019 年 7 月签订"国际货物运输合同",约定由 A 公司将 B 公司的一批啤酒设备从中国的深圳盐田港出口运输到加拿大的多伦多港,交付给收货人。合同中约定:①运费由收货人直接支付到 A 公司指定账户;② A 公司与收货人没有直接合约关系;B 公司作为担保方,确保 A 公司能在规定时间内收到运费;③货物装船后,A 公司向 B 公司交付全套清洁已装船提单/电放单。但是,A 公司作为货运代理人并没有按照约定收到运费,且 B 公司又是一家负债累累的失信被执行人。

【案例分析】

本案例涉及国际货物运输中的托运人、承运人、收货人和担保人等多方法律关系,其中的法律风险主要有以下几点。

(1) A 公司与 B 公司属于业务合作,事前 A 公司没有对 B 公司进行有效的商务调查是导致此次业务风险的第一个因素。如果 A 公司能在事前委托律师进行资信调查,那就很容易发现 B 公司信誉不良的问题。

(2) 合同中约定由国外的收货人支付运费是此次业务风险的第二个因素。A 公司在加拿大多伦多没有分支机构,对收货人的情况一无所知。A 公司不但没有取得收货人同意支付运费的任何书面承诺,而且也不掌握收货人的任何信息资料,不排除存在 B 公司与国外收货人合谋欺诈 A 公司的可能。

（3）合同中约定 B 公司仅仅是运费支付的担保人，这一约定是此项业务风险的第三个因素。在本案中，B 公司作为托运人（货主），完全有义务支付运费，也就是说，A 公司完全可以让 B 公司（货主或托运人）支付运费，而不是让收货人支付运费。如果由 B 公司支付运费的话，在收取运费之前，A 公司可以通过控制提单或者其他有效单据来阻止收货人收取货物，从而让 B 公司先行支付运费。

【结论】

承运人或货运代理人不应当承接不符合交易习惯的业务。承运人或货运代理人在没有收到运费、垫付的费用前，控制提单或者其他贸易单据是避免损失产生的最好手段。同时，承运人或货运代理人还应能够识别合同条款中的隐藏风险。

【案例来源】

盛建明.国际经济法：英文版[M].北京：对外经济贸易大学出版社，2011.

【案例问题】

作为货运代理人，A 公司没有收到运费的主要原因是什么？

5.2　货代纠纷

【知识点】

海上货物运输、货运代理、清关

【案例介绍】

2018 年 11 月初，甲就涉案货物从中国上海运输至加拿大蒙特利尔的货运代理费用向 A 公司询价。甲接受报价后向 A 公司发送了托运物品明细。A 公司与甲确认涉案货物中包含需要熏蒸的实木货物，同时将公司的上海收货地址告知甲。之后甲向 A 公司支付了熏蒸费、商检费（合计人民币 3000 元）；以及海运费、报关费、短驳费、码头费（合计人民币 34450 元）。A 公司陆续完成货物的集港、装箱、订舱事宜。

2018 年 11 月 27 日，涉案货物装船，承运人签发提单，记载收货人及通知人均为 Z3 精品咖啡有限公司、装货港上海、卸货港温哥华、交货地蒙特利尔等信息。甲的儿子乙负责货物在蒙特利尔的清关工作。11 月 30 日，A 公司向甲发送涉案货物熏蒸 / 消毒证书。后经法院与上海海关核实，该证书所涉货物并非本案货物。12 月 23 日，货物到达温哥华。加拿大边境服务局对货物进行了查验，以货物木质包装材料不符合规定、缺少必要的《国际植物保护公约》标识为由，拒绝货物入境。经甲多次与 A 公司沟通后，A 公司确认先将货物退运回中国香港，并以 A 公司香港分公司作为货物退运的收货人。

2019 年 1 月 15 日，乙代甲支付了货物在加拿大的检验费用及从加拿大退运回香港的费用（合计 11235.43 加元）。2 月 19 日，装载涉案货物的船舶从温哥华起运。3 月 12 日，船舶抵达香港。3 月 28 日，A 公司函告甲：务必于次日前确认回运资料并支付仓储费用 7800 港元，否则仓库将对货物进行销毁处理，由甲承担弃货产生的风险和责任。同日，甲回复 A 公司：A 公司反复要求其在多处空白的委托单等资料上签字不合理，A 公司未向其出示完整、规范的文本，因此产生的任何费用及风险都与甲无关。之后，货物在香港被销毁。

结合甲向 A 公司发送的托运产品清单及其购买物品的淘宝记录、付款凭证等证据，涉案货物价值 85249.1 元人民币。甲、乙为本案诉讼支出律师费 50000 元人民币，交通费 6706.7 元人民币，住宿费 3396 元人民币，公证费 7080 元人民币，翻译费 3593.5 元人民币，快递费 71 元人民币。甲、乙以 A 公司提供虚假的熏蒸/消毒证书、未办理符合海关要求的检疫文件、未对货物进行妥善保管等为由提出诉讼请求：判令撤销合同；判令 A 公司向其返还上海至蒙特利尔运费 34450 元人民币、熏蒸费及商检费合计 3000 元人民币、温哥华至香港垫付费用 57237.77 元人民币，赔偿其货物损失 91360.74 元人民币、货物延迟改装修费用及营业收入损失（包括取暖、房租等费用）302869.28 元人民币，给付律师费 50000 元人民币、差旅费 10105 元人民币、翻译费 3593.5 元人民币、公证费 7080 元人民币、打印费 825 元人民币、快递费 71 元人民币。

A 公司辩称，本案不存在法律规定的撤销合同情形；甲、乙及其在目的地的清关公司在货物起运前，未及时向 A 公司告知目的地的清关要求，致使货物未能顺利清关；甲未向 A 公司告知货物的用途、咖啡店开业时间等，A 公司在缔约时无法合理预见咖啡店的营业损失；货物退运回香港后，甲不配合回运，致使货物最终被香港仓库销毁。A 公司对损失的发生不存在过错，对诉讼的各项损失不应承担责任。

【案例分析】

这是一起海上货物运输代理合同纠纷案。在同类案件中，国际货运代理企业经常以其不负责目的地清关事务作为其不履行合同义务的抗辩。

本案从委托事务的合同目的出发，界定国际货运代理企业的合同义务，即国际货运代理企业应及时了解我国及目的地国家或地区检疫法规及政策，使受托货物及包装的熏蒸、检疫行为达到目的地检疫检验的要求。当国际货运代理企业违反上述合同义务时，应根据其过错程度及是否采取了有效措施来综合认定其承担责任的范围，该责任范围包括货物损失、与货物运输相关的损失、与货物相关的预期利益损失及与诉讼相关的损失。

海事法院认为，A 公司接受甲的委托，代其处理涉案货物与海上运输有关的集港、装箱、熏蒸、检疫、订舱、报关、报检等事务，甲与 A 公司之间海上货运代理合同关系成立。依照《中华人民共和国民法典》规定，甲未证明 A 公司在协商订立合同的过程中有欺诈行为，使其在违背真实意思的情况下订立合同，因此，法院对甲主张撤销合同不予支持。乙非涉案海上货运代理合同的相对人，法院对其向 A 公司主张违约责任不予支持。

接下来分析 A 公司是否违反了熏蒸、检疫合同义务。涉案货物虽由乙负责蒙特利尔的清关工作，但 A 公司作为多年从事国际货运代理业务的专业货运代理公司，理应清楚并了解我国及货物目的地国家或地区相关检疫法规及政策，使货物及包装的熏蒸、检疫行为达到我国及目的地国家或地区的标准，从而保证货物在目的地通过检疫检验，实现报关、报检符合相关规定的合同目的。我国海关总署于 2018 年修订的《出境货物木质包装检疫处理管理办法》第四条规定，出境货物木质包装应当按照《出境货物木质包装除害处理方法》列明的检疫除害处理方法实施处理，并按照《出境货物木质包装除害处理标识要求》加施专用标识。A 公司未证明其为涉案货物办理了合法有效的熏蒸/消毒证书，亦未证明涉案货物的木质包装上有符合法律规定的专用标识。A 公司未完成涉案货物及包装的熏蒸检疫合同义务，致使货物在加拿大被查验时，因木质包装材料不符合规定、缺少必要的标识而被拒绝入境，甲的合同目的无法实现，A 公司应承担违约责任。

【结论】

海事法院判决：A 公司向甲给付熏蒸费、商检费、海运费、报关费、短驳费、码头费合计 37450 元人民币，甲在加拿大垫付的费用 57237.77 元人民币，货物损失 85249.1 元人民币，翻译费 3593.5 元人民币，公证费 7080 元人民币，快递费 71 元人民币，差旅费 10102.7 元人民币，律师费 25000 元人民币；驳回甲的其他诉讼请求；驳回乙对 A 公司的诉讼请求。各方当事人均未提起上诉，该判决已发生法律效力。

【案例来源】

董世华. 一例海上货运代理合同纠纷案件评析[J]. 世界海运，2020，43（11）：54-56.

【案例问题】

结合案例内容，谈一谈你对海事法院判决的看法。

5.3　船舶碰撞纠纷

【知识点】

国际海运、租船合同、船舶碰撞、《海牙规则》

【案例介绍】

2019 年 3 月 2 日，马士基旗下的"SAFMARINE NOKWANDA"号集装箱船在釜山集装箱码头靠泊时与星旗号下一艘已停泊的"TIANJIN"号集装箱船相撞，导致"TIANJIN"号货物遭受严重损失，众多集装箱倒塌甚至被压碎，船体结构也遭到严重损坏。"TIANJIN"号在 3 月 2 日到达釜山前曾挂靠天津港、青岛港、宁波港、上海港，船上有众多中国货代货主的集装箱。"TIANJIN"号准备前往巴拿马运河、牙买加的金斯敦港、美国的萨凡纳港、查尔斯顿港和杰克逊维尔港。

【案例分析】

这是一起因船舶在港口靠泊不当引发的责任案例，应当按照相关规则进行责任的划分和承担。

"船舶互撞责任条款"是货方偿还船方费用的条款。承运人与货主签订提单或租船合同时附加"船舶互撞责任条款"以保护承运人能够按照《海牙规则》取得利益。该责任条款规定，如船舶由于他船疏忽及本船船长、船员、引航员或承运人的雇佣人在驾驶船舶或管理船舶中的行为疏忽或不履行职责（免责事项）而与他船碰撞，则本船所载货物的所有人应承担补偿承运人的一切损失或对他船的赔偿责任。

但由于一般提单均订有承运人对船长、船员在航行或管理船舶上的行为或疏忽的免责条款，因此货主不能向其承运人索赔，而只能向对方责任船方索赔。

按照《1910年统一船舶碰撞若干法律规定的国际公约》的规定，当船舶碰撞互有责任时，两船上的货物损失由过失船舶各按过失程度比例赔偿，并分摊承运船的一部分损失。承运人为了维持自身的利益，在提单中加入了"船舶互撞责任条款"，规定货主应向承运人退还他从对方船获得的承运过失比例的赔款。伦敦保险协会的保险条款规定，对于货物所有人（被保险人）应该向承运人退回的损失，可由保险人负责赔偿。

【结论】

本案中马士基的"SAFMARINE NOKWANDA"号集装箱船与星旗号下的"TIANJIN"号集装箱船相撞，"TIANJIN"号的货物损失和船体损失由"SAFMARINE NOKWANDA"号负全部责任。"TIANJIN"号应及时通知货主集装箱受损情况。按照"船舶互撞责任条款"规定，购买保险的货主在补偿了"TIANJIN"号的损失后，还可以向保险公司索赔。而未购买保险的货主就只能自己赔偿船方的这部分损失。

【案例来源】

马祯.由海运事故谈国际货物运输中保险的重要性[J].中国经贸导刊（中），2019（7）：53-55.

【案例问题】

《海牙规则》对承运人利益的保护有哪些具体规定？

5.4　中欧班列运输

【知识点】

国际货物运输、"一带一路"倡议、电子数据交换、无纸化运输

【案例介绍】

2017 年，中国、白俄罗斯、德国、俄罗斯、波兰、哈萨克斯坦、蒙古国等国家的铁路公司在中欧班列运输合作上达成广泛共识，成立联合工作组。在中欧班列运输联合工作组第一次会议（中国郑州）和第二次会议（白俄罗斯明斯克）的成果基础上，中国铁路总公司作为主办方，分别于 2018 年 3 月和 8 月召开了中欧班列七国信息协作专家工作组第一次会议（中国苏州）和第二次会议（中国成都），工作组围绕中欧班列电子数据交换和无纸化运输等核心问题进行了深入交流和广泛讨论，共同商议了中欧班列信息化工作计划和双边信息交换机制等内容。2019年 3 月，工作组第三次会议在中国西安成功召开，继续共商中欧班列运输和发展相关事宜。

【案例分析】

本案例主要介绍了"一带一路"倡议下的中欧班列高效协作机制。这一机制的运行和落实极大地促进了中国与沿线国家货运的便利性。

（1）中国铁路国际联运电子数据交换现状。中国铁路总公司在国内国际联运电子信息全程采集基础上，自主研发了国际联运电子数据交换平台，提供国际货协运单信息指令、列车编组确报等与相邻国家之间的报文交换服务。中国铁路总公司分别与俄罗斯、哈萨克斯坦、蒙古国的铁路公司签订货物运输电子数据交换协议或审

查文本协议，并协调了工作机制，制订了工作计划，同时明确了电子数据交换内容和技术要求。以中俄、中哈、中蒙国际联运电子数据交换为基础，中国铁路总公司将陆续开展与白俄罗斯、波兰、德国等非"两临"国家之间的电子信息交换工作，以实现中欧班列电子数据两两交换的全覆盖。

（2）中欧班列无纸化进程的难点。中欧班列全程无纸化的实现，需要中欧班列沿线各国之间实现国际货协运单信息指令、列车编组确报等报文的电子数据交换。因中欧班列运输具有跨越多国、运距远、历时长、口岸作业复杂等作业特点和难点，要实现中欧班列全程无纸化运输，在各承运国意愿相同的基础上还需要克服几项重要技术难点，主要包括双边国家数据共享电子签名及法律效力的互认、非"两临"国家基于互联网的信息共享安全机制、添附文件的无纸化技术研究、各国法律对无纸化的要求等。

【结论】

中欧班列的顺利运行需要沿线各国铁路、海关之间的高效协作，中欧班列无纸化运输及货物电子信息共享，将大幅降低运输成本、提高运输效率，同时也将极大地推动沿线国家及地区的经济发展。此外，中欧班列将提升全球的国际运输能力，对推动构建人类命运共同体具有重要意义。中欧班列的顺利运行也充分说明中国"一带一路"倡议和"共商、共建、共享"全球治理理念的正确性。

【案例来源】

刘洋.中欧班列全程无纸化运输研究与分析[C]//第十五届中国智能交通年会科技论文集（2），2020：148-151.

【案例问题】

试说明中欧班列无纸化运输和货物电子信息共享对国际货物运输的促进作用。

5.5 FOB 责任认定

【知识点】

国际货物运输、托运人、承运人、货运代理、FOB、正本提单

【案例介绍】

原告南洋商贸按照被告青岛万达提供的收货通知，将涉案货物交由其运输。青岛万达作为另一被告万达运通（货运代理公司）的代理人签发了涉案货物的全套正本提单。该批货物提单载明：托运人为南洋商贸，承运人为万达运通，青岛万达为万达运通的授权签单代理人。

为完成上述货物的运输事宜，被告将货物交付作为实际承运人的德翔海运公司运输，托运人为青岛万达，收货人为寰亚国际物流公司（物流代理公司）。南洋商贸为顺利出运该批货物，向青岛万达支付了货物的起运港杂费。涉案货物装船时的价值共计 324055 美元。诉讼中，南洋商贸请求法院判令两被告赔偿货物损失1977869.69 元人民币及利息。

两被告辩称，原、被告之间不存在海上货物运输的合同关系。本案涉及的成交方式为船上交货（FOB），订舱人应当是南洋商贸的买方或该买方指定的代理人；由于寰亚国际物流公司涉嫌盗窃、诈骗等原因，因此原告南洋商贸在本案中负有不可推卸的责任。两被告当庭陈述，其已将涉案货物交付寰亚国际物流公司，且涉案货物全套正本提单均未收回，目前为南洋商贸所持有。被告主张，寰亚国际物流公司涉嫌刑事犯罪，已向警方报警。

【案例分析】

本案例涉及国际货物运输中的多方当事人及他们之间的合同关系,具体分析如下。

(1)万达运通与南洋商贸之间存在海上货物运输合同关系。南洋商贸在一审中提交的对账单、汇款凭证和发票能够证实,其向青岛万达支付了涉案货物在起运港所发生的费用。因此,可以认定南洋商贸将货物交给了青岛万达。青岛万达作为万达运通的代理人,接收货物后签发了提单,南洋商贸是正本提单上记载的托运人。

以上事实表明,南洋商贸符合《中华人民共和国海商法》(以下简称海商法)中关于"第二种交货托运人"的定义。万达运通却主张,本案货物买卖合同的价格条款为FOB,货物的买方委托寰亚国际物流公司订舱。万达运通主张的上述事实,仅导致南洋商贸不符合海商法中关于"第一种契约托运人"的定义。但由于南洋商贸符合"第二种交货托运人"的定义,因此南洋商贸仍为涉案海上运输合同的托运人,与作为承运人的万达运通之间存在海上运输合同关系。

(2)被告万达运通应当承担赔偿责任。依照我国海商法第四十六条的规定,承运人对集装箱装运的货物的责任期间,是指从装货港接收货物时起至卸货港交付货物时止,货物处于承运人掌管之下的全部期间;在承运人的责任期间,货物发生灭失或者损坏,除本节另有规定外,承运人应当负赔偿责任。涉案提单项下的货物运抵目的港后,万达运通在涉案货物全套正本提单均由南洋商贸持有的情形下,指示实际承运人将货物交付案外人寰亚国际物流公司,导致涉案货物被他人占有和控制。万达运通的上述行为,违反了我国海商法第七十一条关于提单是承运人据以交付货物的保证的规定。

万达运通作为承运人,违反了凭正本提单交付货物的义务,使得南洋商贸对提单项下的货物失去了控制权。因此,万达运通应当赔偿南洋商贸由此产生的货物损失。万达运通不能以寰亚国际物流公司涉嫌盗窃、诈骗,南洋商贸的买方信息不真实为由,免除其在海上货物运输合同项下,凭正本提单交付货物的义务。

【结论】

结合案例内容和陈述事实可知，万达运通应当依照法律规定赔偿南洋商贸的损失。本案的裁决对国内卖方及承运人的启示是：无论采用何种贸易术语，以及如何操作租船订舱事宜，在签发正本提单的情况下，只有凭正本提单交付货物才能免除法律风险。采用 FOB 条款订立国际贸易合同时，卖方若放弃在正本提单中记载为"托运人"的权利，则必须持有货物的全套正本提单，这是国内卖方防范国际贸易风险的法律防线。

【案例来源】

刘晓亮，崔静坤. 从一则案例看 FOB 下无单放货的风险与防范［J］. 对外经贸实务，2020（12）：69–71.

【案例问题】

（1）运用 FOB 条款订立国际货物运输合同时应当注意哪些事项？
（2）当事人运用正本提单交货应履行哪些法定义务？

5.6　无单放货

【知识点】

国际货物运输、货代合同、提单、无单放货

【案例介绍】

2018 年 11 月，重庆 ABC 实业有限公司（以下简称 ABC 实业）以船上交货（FOB）术语与土耳其买方订立 8 万美元的货物出口合同，付款方式为：30% 预付款，

70%尾款见提单扫描件付清。货物生产完成后，买方指定上海港（装运港）D货代公司安排运输。此外，ABC实业在订舱时和D货代公司特别强调此票货物尾款还没有收回，如果签发货代单，则D货代公司不能将船公司提单交给买方。2019年1月5日，买方反馈信息说明，其已经在目的港海关仓库见到货物，并发现产品质量不符合合同约定，要求降价20%才肯付款收货，否则将拒绝收货。与此同时，D货代公司与买方都不能提供货物仍在目的港海关仓库的证据。货物到底是在目的港海关仓库还是买方自己仓库仍需调查。不可否认的是，买方在没有支付尾款且从ABC实业取得正本货代提单的情况下，提前看到了货物，并在没有任何第三方检验机构检验报告的情况下，单方面以质量问题为由要求降价，甚至以拒付进行威胁，给ABC实业安全收汇带来了较大的风险。

【案例分析】

上述案例主要介绍了买方在未取得货物的情况下，以在海关仓库看到货物质量不符合合同约定为由，要求卖方降价，以及由此产生的争议。

本案构成无单放货。在本案中，D货代公司辩称货物仍在目的港海关仓库，仍处在目的港货代控制之下，但是却不能提供相应证据（如由目的港海关监管仓库或保税仓库出具的存货证明）。

另外，买方反映的验货不合格问题证明其实质接触过货物。但是本案中的载明运输货物的正本货代提单却一直在ABC实业手里，说明目的港货代公司在未收回正本货代提单的情况下，就对货物进行了拆箱，甚至放货给买方，这一事实符合无单放货的定义，所以本案构成无单放货，相关责任方需要承担相应的责任。

【结论】

卖方想要避免无单放货，可以要求买方指定货代与其签订国际货物运输代理合同。签订合同后，指定货代就需要承担合同中约定的责任，安排国际货物运输时就会更加谨慎与尽职，从而有效防范无单放货行为发生的风险。同时，签订国际货物运输代理合同，也可以有效避免发生争议时提单上的格式化条款对指定货代的某些行为免责，在仲裁或诉讼时对卖方也就更为有利。

【案例来源】

宋娟娟，刘康. 海运出口货物无单放货风险分析及防范：以重庆 ABC 实业有限公司一则被无单放货业务为例[J]. 对外经贸实务，2019（3）：54–57.

【案例问题】

本案中对无单放货的责任是如何认定的？有哪些具体规则？

第 **6** 章

国际贸易支付

6.1　出口电汇结算风险

【知识点】

国际贸易支付、西联汇款、电汇、电放提单

【案例介绍】

2014 年，义乌服装出口商 A 公司以成本、保险加运费（CIF）价格术语，向尼日利亚进口商 B 公司出口服装，总价为 2 万美元，采用装运前电汇 25%，装运后见提单传真件后电汇 75% 的方式支付货款，并使用西联汇款平台电汇，电放提单交货。B 公司使用西联汇款支付 5000 美元后，A 公司按照合同约定按期发货，并及时传真提单复印件给 B 公司。B 公司告知 A 公司，因尼日利亚外汇管制较严，每次汇款上限是 5000 美元，余款 15000 美元将分三次电汇。A 公司在义乌建行西联汇款代办处查询后，在得知尾款首批 5000 美元已汇到的同时，授权承运人可电放货物，B 公司立刻凭提单传真件提取了全部货物。数日后，A 公司拟到义乌建行西联汇款代办处一次性提取尾款 15000 美元时，被告知 B 公司已要求退汇了，A 公司因此损失了 75% 的货款。

【案例分析】

本案例介绍了因货物进口商撤销电汇导致出口商货款损失的事实。由此可以看出，在国际贸易支付实践中，电汇支付存在一定的风险，出口商应事先做好风险防范。

（1）进口商撤汇的风险。第三方跨境电汇平台办理汇款到账速度非常快，一般十几分钟就能到账。但是，如果收款人不及时将款项提走，则汇款人可以随时申请退汇，并且退汇时不需要征得收款人的同意。本案例中义乌的 A 公司从西联汇款代办处查询到货款汇到后，未及时提款，给尼日利亚的 B 公司骗取货物提供了方便。这一点也是广大中小贸易企业常面临的信用困境。

（2）"装运后见提单传真件电汇（T/T）+ 电放提单"方式造成的风险。装运后见提单传真件支付方式本身就给出口商利用货权约束进口商付款带来了较大的风险，这种方式需要配合由出口商指定承运人的价格术语才能降低货损风险。而电放提单提货方式使得进口商仅凭提单传真件就可从承运人处提货，出口商向进口商传真提单以要求其电汇货款的行为，给进口商先行提货创造了条件。

（3）小额出口贸易使得出口商维权成本过高。利用第三方跨境电汇平台办理电汇货款的外贸交易往往贸易额较小。当进口商违约拒绝付款时，出口商依照进出口合同维权的成本经常会超过贸易额本身，这使得出口商不得不放弃海外维权行为。

（4）电汇支付方式下出口商能否安全收回货款主要取决于进口商的信用。为了避免收汇过程中出现不必要的风险，选择一个资信状况好的进口商尤为重要。因此，出口商签订合同前，必须对进口商的资信情况有所了解。例如，在互联网条件下，出口商可以通过进口商的企业网站或企业黄页信息、进口商的账户行等进行资信调查。对于大客户还可以采用实地走访的方式或委托中国出口信用保险公司进行调查。对于调查的信息和结果，出口商要建立客户信息库，详细记录客户的基本信息，特别是要记录其信保额度和回款情况。对记录在案的资信良好的客户，出口商就可以在选择合同付款方式时适当接受风险承担方面的让步；对于信用较差的客户，则应重点关注，坚持原则，尽量不留下风险隐患。

出口商在对进口商的资信程度及资产情况进行调查评估后，可以根据合同货值和进口商资金流通状况，在合同中适当要求进口商在发货前通过电汇预付部分货款，并且预付比例越高，出口商遭受损失的可能性和程度就越小。在实际业务中，出口商通常可以要求进口商预付 20%～30% 的合同货值，如果进口商没有充分的理由就拒绝预先电汇部分货款，并要求在到货后电汇，出口商就要高度关注潜在风险，要在价格术语和运输方式的选择方面做好足够的风险防范工作。

【结论】

采用银行传统电汇结算方式存在汇款人申请退汇的风险，第三方跨境电汇结算方式也存在一定的支付风险。出口商应加强对进口商的资信调查，并建立客户信息库，做到事先规避风险。同时，出口商应要求进口商预先电汇一定比例的货款，以降低可能的损失。

【案例来源】

孟亮．出口商在采用电汇结算方式下的风险及防控措施分析［J］.对外经贸实务，2016（7）：64-67.

【案例问题】

（1）试比较出口商和进口商在采用电汇结算方式时所面临的不同风险。

（2）试了解目前跨境电商平台的应用规则与相关法律规定。

6.2 贸易结算方式的选择

【知识点】

国际贸易支付、结算方式、信用证、跟单托收、单证不符

【案例介绍】

2020年5月10日，青岛远大贸易公司（以下简称远大公司）与沙特阿拉伯的Almarran公司签订一份纺织品出口合约。由于Almarran公司是大客户，长期从远大公司批量采购床上用品等，远大公司为了给客户提供融资便利，在合同中拟采用远期信用证结算方式。同时，考虑自身资金周转实际情况和货款安全性，远大公司要

求 Almarran 预付 30% 货款作为定金。最终合同的支付方式为：电汇 30% 预付款，其余 70% 货款采用信用证结算，期限为 90 天。

2020 年 6 月 10 日，远大公司收到 Almarran 开来的信用证。信用证对提单做了如下要求："直达提单必须由阳明海运签发，整箱运输。该提单必须有纺织品字样、集装箱编号、注明是 20 英尺还是 40 英尺、铅封号、总包装或卷数、信用证编号、毛重"。由于两地港口之间没有直达船，必然会出现单证不符的情况，远大公司只好联系 Almarran 公司要求其修改信用证，Almarran 公司业务员以修改信用证成本较高和双方长期合作为由，声称跟单托收也可以，公司保证付款赎单。虽然多次商讨未果，但是考虑到双方的长期合作关系，且公司已经投保中信保，远大公司继续与 Almarran 公司沟通。远大公司在 Almarran 公司再次电汇 50% 余款，从而保证了自己的生产成本后，为 Almarran 公司发运了货物。随后，由于单证不符，远大公司将信用证等单据交银行做了跟单托收，并回收了剩余货款。

【案例分析】

本案例涉及国际货物支付与结算方式的选择及其风险的预防措施。具体分析如下。

（1）结算方式的类型。在本案中，合同履行中的突发状况导致合同结算方式发生变更，由此涉及了多种结算方式的使用。买卖双方在签订合同时，采用了电汇（T/T）和信用证（L/C）两种结算方式，其中，T/T 属于汇付的一种业务类型。在实际业务中，电汇是由付款方通过银行，使用电报等电子手段将款项支付给收款方。其手续简单、速度快、费用低，属于商业信用，当进口方资信好、双方关系密切时，这是一种理想的结算方式。信用证是开证银行向受益人做出的一份承诺，保证在符合信用证条款的条件下，凭规定单据有条件付款。案例中的合同使用的是远期信用证，但由于单证不符，又使用了托收结算方式。托收是指出口方开具以进口方为付款人的汇票，委托出口地银行通过其在进口方所在地的分行或代理行向进口方收取货款的一种结算方式，分为光票托收和跟单托收。案例中使用的是跟单托收，即出口商先发货，进口商后付款。

（2）不同结算方式的风险。汇付，属于商业信用，依赖买方的信用状况。除了100%的提前电汇，其他汇付方式都可能面临难以收回货款的风险，尤其是货到付款的电汇风险最大。托收也属于商业信用，出口商发货后，开立汇票连同商业单据交银行委托收款。在此过程中，银行只提供服务，不提供信用担保。是否能够安全收回货款也完全取决于买方的资信状况，单独使用时风险大。信用证付款是以银行信用代替商业信用，开证行承担第一性付款责任，解决了进出口双方互相不信任的问题，是国际贸易中相对安全的支付方式。但信用证付款手续烦琐、费用较高，对制单的要求严格，即使采用即期信用证，出口商也可能会面临因难以做到的"软条款"或者各种原因的单证不符而导致开证行拒付的情况。

（3）案例中的出口商远大公司无疑有着较强的风险意识。第一，签订合同时，远大公司使用了"前电汇 + 远期信用证"方式。由于作为长期客户的 Almarran 公司要求远期结算，考虑到信用证是国际贸易中相对安全的结算方式，因此远大公司选择了远期信用证，而非其他货到付款方式，同时要求了30%的预付货款；第二，履行合同时，远大公司在面临突发的单证不符可能时，改为采取"前电汇 + 跟单托收"方式。在进口方拒绝改证后，为了保障货款安全，远大公司再次要求进口方汇付余款的50%，确保了货物的生产成本。这时即使剩余款项无法收回，也能保证此次出口不亏损。

【结论】

国际贸易支付通常使用汇付、托收、信用证及国际保理等方式。虽然在实务中可以选择的结算方式很多，但没有哪一种结算方式绝对安全。企业可以根据业务情况恰当组合，还可以投保出口信用保险，同时要注重匹配合同的交易条件。对卖方来说，买方的信用状况和资信状况对其选择结算方式及管控结算风险来说至关重要。

【案例来源】

王丽.从一则案例看国际贸易结算方式选择和风险防范[J].对外经贸实务，2021（9）：85–88.

【案例问题】

（1）试分析出口贸易风险的影响因素。

（2）试比较不同的国际贸易结算方式及其风险。

6.3 信用证使用规则

【知识点】

国际贸易支付、信用证、单单一致、单证一致

【案例介绍】

2019年3月，上海A公司和美国B公司签订了价值为100000美元的电子产品出口合同，规定贸易条件为空运到纽约成本加运费（CFR NEW YORK BY AIR），支付方式选用"不可撤销"的即期信用证，装运方式为次月从上海通过空运的方式到达美国纽约。

签订合同后，美国B公司在纽约当地开了一张信用证，通知行和议付行为上海的一家银行，信用证上的价格术语是"CNF NEW YORK"。上海A公司收到信用证之后，按照合同规定将货物发送出去，准备妥当信用证所需的各种单据，并且办理议付手续。但是上海议付行在将各种单据资料寄送到纽约开证行时，却收到了纽约开证行的拒收通知，原因是单证不符。上海A公司的商业发票上的价格术语是成本加运费"CFR NEW YORK"，而信用证上的价格术语是"CNF NEW YORK"，两者贸

易术语不同。上海 A 公司知晓此事后，立即向美国开证行提出异议，要求美国 B 公司按照合同规定支付货款或者进行赔偿。与此同时，上海 A 公司联系货物承运人，欲撤销发运的货物，但是为时已晚，货物已经被发运。美国 B 公司坚决不赔偿损失，而纽约开证行又认为单证不符，拒绝支付款项，最终上海 A 公司遭受了巨大的损失。

【案例分析】

这是一个典型的信用证使用中的"单证不符"案例。商业发票上的价格术语是"CFR NEW YORK"，与信用证上的价格术语"CNF NEW YORK"不符，导致进口商开证行拒付货款，从而给出口商造成经济损失。

（1）单证不一致的风险。信用证有三个特点，分别是信用证交易的独立性、信用证交易的单据性和银行作为第三方提供信用。第一，信用证交易具有独立性，信用证的产生源于进出口双方所达成的合同，但是信用证又独立于合同，不受进出口双方合同的约束。第二，信用证交易的单据只要符合"单单一致，单证一致"，银行就会付款。第三，银行作为第三方与买卖双方没有实质性的关联，只是提供信用。无论单据是否在有效期内，货物是否已经运送至进口地，只要符合《跟单信用证统一惯例》（UCP600）的"单单一致，单证一致"，银行就会提供付款服务。本案例中的上海 A 公司遭受损失的第一个原因就是单证不符。上海 A 公司没有做好认真审单和验单的工作。上海 A 公司在收到信用证以后，没有及时将美国 B 公司的信用证与自己的单据进行对照，没有审核单证是否一致，忽视了单据的审核工作，给自己造成了巨大的经济损失。

（2）不熟悉空运贸易。运输方式不同及各国的贸易法律法规不同，给进出口双方带来了潜在的风险。在本案例中，由于上海 A 公司并不熟悉空运的特点及相关法律法规，不了解空运方式下信用证的结算流程，因此上海 A 公司遭受了不可挽回的损失。另外，上海 A 公司使用的是标准的贸易术语，但是美国 B 公司使用的是过去的贸易术语。虽然 CFR 和 CNF 只是成本加运费在不同时期的不同表达，但是其本质是相同的，因此上海 A 公司就没有过多考虑两种贸易术语的不同。殊不知，在国际贸易中，细微的差别就会造成巨大的损失。

【结论】

在国际贸易支付实践中，开证行应认真做好审查信用证的工作，出口方在收到信用证之后，需要将信用证与合同进行对照，认真审查单据，保证"单单一致，单证一致"。此外，进出口双方都应熟悉国际货物运输方式的特点和相关规则。

【案例来源】

曹云.从空运案例分析国际贸易中信用证风险与防范[J].对外经贸实务，2021（6）：78–81.

【案例问题】

试分析信用证的法律特点与交易规则。

6.4　备用信用证与开证行付款义务

【知识点】

备用信用证、开证行、申请人、受益人、汇票、《国际备用证惯例》

【案例介绍】

英国甲银行应申请人乙要求开出以日本丙公司为受益人的备用信用证，该备用信用证要求受益人用四张汇票分四期支款，支款时须提供申请人违约的如下声明："因为在到期日申请人乙没有向受益人丙支付四张汇票中的一张所载明的金额，因此，所开立汇票的金额代表开证申请人应该支付而未付的金额。"

前三期，申请人乙于备用信用证分期支款日前，直接向受益人丙支付了应付的分期支款金额。因此，丙无须在备用信用证项下开立特殊的分期支款汇票。在分期支款第四张汇票到期后，申请人没有像前三次那样如期付款，因此受益人向开证行提交了备用信用证所要求的违约声明书和汇票，以便在备用信用证项下向甲银行索取申请人所欠款项，但甲银行收到单据后拒绝付款。

【案例分析】

本案例涉及备用信用证的开证行、申请人、受益人，以及关于备用信用证的两个国际惯例。本案例的争议主要源于两个国际惯例的侧重点不同。

（1）《跟单信用证统一惯例》（UCP600）主要应用于贸易领域，大多针对普通商业信用证。按照UCP600第32条规定，如信用证规定在指定的时间段内分期支款或分期发运，任何一期未按信用证规定期限支取或发运时，信用证对该期及以后各期均告失效。

（2）《国际备用证惯例》（ISP98）专门为备用信用证提供了独立的规则。备用信用证属于银行信用，对受益人来说是备用于开证申请人发生毁约时，取得补偿的一种方式。

【结论】

由于本案中的当事人没有指明依照哪种惯例规范备用证，因此应以《国际备用证惯例》规定为准，即甲银行应当履行付款义务。

【案例来源】

王海英.国际经济法案例教程［M］.2版.北京：北京大学出版社，2012.

【案例问题】

在国际贸易支付中，备用信用证适用哪些规则？

6.5　贸易支付与 UCP600 规则

【知识点】

国际贸易支付、自由议付信用证、《跟单信用证统一惯例》（UCP600）

【案例介绍】

2008 年 7 月 22 日，在中国香港上市的内地某股份制银行厦门分行应厦门一买方客户的要求开立信用证，为一宗"数量为 45000 湿公吨（WMTs）、卖方可选择 +/–10%（ +/–10% at seller′s option）、价格条件为成本加运费 / 指定港船上交货（CFR/FOB）、每公吨 183 美元的铁矿石国际买卖合同"，开立了金额为 8235000 美元的信用证，信用证适用《跟单信用证统一惯例》（UCP600），受益人为一家新加坡公司，该信用证为自由议付信用证，但是信用证又规定见单后 90 天付款。同时，信用证规定交单付款地为厦门。

此后，受益人分别于 2008 年 7 月 19 日和 7 月 23 日在印度将 44500 吨货物装运发往中国内地。船上货物价值 7185105.43 美元。货物于 8 月 2 日到达广西防城港并于次日卸货。7 月 30 日，受益人将单据提交给议付行并要求获得付款，8 月 4 日，议付行将单据转递给开证行，开证行于 8 月 6 日收到信用证单据。

此后开证行分别于 8 月 11 日、8 月 12 日和 8 月 13 日发出三道电文，后两份电文否定了第一份电文接受单据、同意付款的内容，并在第三份电文中以受益人提交单据存在不符点为由拒绝付款。第一个不符点是信用证金额问题，受益人提款金额为 7185105.43 美元，而信用证金额为 8235000 美元，受益人提取的数额低于信用证规定的金额（10% 增减）下限。第二个和第三个不符点是货物数量问题，信用证中写的是"45000 公吨、卖方可选择 +/–10%"，开证行认为信用证中的

"45000公吨"是"45000干公吨"，而单据描述的货物数量"44500湿公吨"等于40017.5干公吨，低于信用证规定的货物数量（10%增减）下限。第四个不符点是关于货物价值的问题，开证行认为即使对价格进行调整，货物价值仍不符合信用证所允许的增减范围。8月14日，议付行代表受益人表示不能接受开证行的拒付理由。但是在那个时间段铁矿石价格出现下跌，在此背景下，买卖双方就铁矿石价格纠纷进行协商。2008年9月22日，卖方最终被迫同意降价，将价格从每吨183美元降到每吨128美元。因此货物的价值大约降低到5122240美元。双方签署了降价备忘录。

新加坡受益人遭此损失后，在香港特区高等法院起诉厦门开证行，其理由为：开证行不能以之后的两份电文否定之前的第一份接受单据、同意付款电文的内容，后面的两份电文是没有法律效力的。因此受益人向开证行索赔降价差额2062865.43美元。

厦门开证行提出自己的拒付是合理的，且以本案各方当事人均非香港当事人、本案交易发生在中国内地和新加坡之间为由，提出了不方便管辖抗辩。

2010年5月3日，香港特区高等法院判决开证行拒付不当，开证行应赔偿受益人所遭受的损失。

【案例分析】

本案例是因信用证受益人利益受损而产生的诉讼，开证行和受益人有不同的主张和诉求，香港特区高等法院支持了受益人的主张。结合本案的判决，具体分析如下。

（1）受益人的主张：受益人认为本案事实适用UCP600第14条、第15条和第16条的规定。香港特区高等法院也详细引述了UCP600的前述各条规定。法官注意到，开证行在本案中一共发出三次电文。法官认为一旦开证行发出电文接受单据并同意付款，开证行即受其约束并具有向受益人承兑信用证的义务。开证行只有一次提出拒付并指出不符点的机会。

（2）开证行的主张：开证行于8月13日发出的第三道电文是本案唯一的一份拒

付电文，该电文给出的不符点和拒付理由是："仍在 5 个银行工作日内，开证行有权根据 UCP600 第 14 条 d 款决定单据是否相符。"

（3）香港特区高等法院的判决：一审判决驳回开证行律师中止案件审理的请求，同时判决开证行须向受益人支付 2062865.43 美元，以及依照美元基准利率加百分之一的标准，从 2008 年 11 月 9 日直至判决之日的利息。此后的利息将按照判决执行期间的利率进行计算。

【结论】

本案开证行在进行交单、审单，做出拒付等操作程序中存在明显问题，这些问题会给开证行和开证申请人带来潜在的风险。因此，准确理解《跟单信用证统一惯例》（UCP600）规则，特别是 UCP600 第 14 条、第 15 条和第 16 条的有关解释是至关重要的。

【案例来源】

http：//ielaw.uibe.edu.cn/fgal/gwal/19123.htm ［2022–04–25］.

【案例问题】

（1）试阐述《跟单信用证统一惯例》（UCP600）的基本内容。
（2）试分析 UCP600 在国际贸易支付中的地位与作用。

6.6　国际贸易支付与国际保理业务

【知识点】

国际贸易支付、国际保理、进口保理商、出口保理商、承兑交单

【案例介绍】

2013年3月，中国荣华家电公司（以下简称荣华公司）首次打开了拉美哥伦比亚市场的大门，与Costa Porto公司（以下简称Costa公司）商洽出口电磁厨具业务。Costa公司希望以90天内承兑交单方式（D/A at 90 days）结算，荣华公司考虑到这是双方第一次打交道，采用D/A承兑交单方式风险太大，且付款时间长，但又不想失去开发拉美市场的机会，于是提出办理国际保理业务。荣华公司随即向中国银行广东省某分行（以下简称中行）申请办理出口保理业务，中行在哥伦比亚选择了一家银行作为进口保理商。

2013年4月20日，荣华公司在获得了进口保理商核准的28万美元的信用额度后，当即与中行签订公开无追索权的出口保理协议，并与Costa公司签订价值25万美元的出口合同。4月28日，荣华公司在发货后，立即向出口保理商申请融资，出口保理商预付荣华公司20万美元。7月28日为付款到期日，当天Costa公司通过进口保理商发来质量争议通知，以货品质量有问题为由拒付货款，进口保理商将此视为贸易纠纷而免除了坏账担保义务。中行立即向出口商传达该争议内容，希望进出口双方协商解决。于是荣华公司向Costa公司提出提供质量检验证明的要求，对方未能提供，荣华公司认为对方拒付理由不成立，并进一步了解到对方拒付的实际原因是Costa公司的销售商破产，货物被银行扣押，Costa公司无法收回货款。在发票付款到期日后的90天赔付期内，进口保理商仍未付款，中行要求荣华公司返还预付货款，荣华公司认为其已经将发票等票据卖给了中行，因而拒绝返还，进口商不付款的责任应由中行承担。2014年12月5日，出口商委托进口保理商在哥伦比亚起诉进口商，但进口保理商出于自身利益方面的考虑，对协助出口商解决纠纷的态度十分消极，最终出口商败诉，出口商与出口保理商皆承担了风险损失。

【案例分析】

本案例介绍了出口商与进口商之间的贸易支付纠纷，主要涉及国际保理业务的基本环节，以及办理国际保理业务时，出口商、出口保理商所面临的风险和进口商、进口保理商应承担的责任。

（1）风险问题。在本案中，进口商声称货物有质量问题，并以此为由拒付货款，进口保理商认为这是贸易纠纷，免除了自己的坏账担保偿付义务。此外，中行与荣华公司签订的是无追索权的保理协议，在无追索权的保理业务中，当出口保理商在应收账款到期日无法得到进口保理商偿付时，是不能向债权人（出口商）行使追索权的。因此，如果出口保理商未事先在保理协议中就贸易纠纷下的追索权与出口商达成共识，那么出口保理商就要承担国外拒付的风险。在本案例中，由于出口商就质量问题与进口商交涉未果，并在法庭上败诉，因此最终出口商不得不承担了余款未能收回的损失。

（2）质量争议。在本案中，对于引发贸易纷争的货品质量问题是否存在，买卖双方各执一词。Costa 公司提出货品存在质量问题，但却未能提供相关的质量检验证明；而荣华公司查明的进口商拒付的理由实际却是销售商破产导致进口商货款无法收回。本案中的质量问题并未得到核实，进口保理商仅凭一面之词就认定有贸易纠纷而免除了自己的坏账担保义务，由此可见，进口商很可能存在履约瑕疵，而出口商与出口保理商却因此遭受损失。

（3）进口保理商责任。在本案中，作为出口商的诉讼代理人，进口保理商在诉讼过程中协助出口商的态度消极，显而易见其并不想打赢官司，因为如果官司赢了，进口保理商就要履行付款的责任，而基于进口商偿付困难的现实情况，最后很可能要由进口保理商自己承担货款损失。本案中的进口保理商过多地关注自己的利益而非自己的信誉，说明其资信状况不佳，未能尽好保理商的义务。

综合以上三方面的分析来看，国际保理业务中的一个主要风险来自贸易纠纷。贸易纠纷引发的风险对于相关当事人，特别是出口商和出口保理商来说，都是应该事先加以防范的。

【结论】

国际保理业务原本是在赊销、承兑交单等付款方式下，帮助进出口商解决在国际货物贸易过程中因互不了解、互不信任而影响贸易往来的问题，使出口商降低收汇风险，安全取得融资。但如果出口商、出口保理商事先未做好相应的信用风险防范工作，就还是可能会产生进口商拒付的风险。因此，即使出口商使用国际保理业务进行结算，也应做好风险防范工作，谨慎行事才是关键。

【案例来源】

韩余静.从一起贸易纠纷案透析国际保理业务风险及防范要点[J].对外经贸实务，2015（11）：81-83.

【案例问题】

国际保理业务存在哪些法律风险？

Chapter 1

Globalization Strategy of Multinational Corporations

1.1 BP's Strategic Planning for US Market

Related Knowledge

Multinational corporations; Strategic planning; Eclectic paradigm of international production

Case Description

British Petroleum (BP) is one of multinational corporation that dominates the global petroleum industry. It owns the locational advantages and the ownership advantages in multiple aspects including capital, technology, corporate management, and marketing, and could also bring its internal advantages into full play in the transnational operation relying on its strong ability in full integration. Relying on its whole production chain from oil field exploitation to final production of petrochemical products, BP could acquire all the intermediate products it needs from internal transactions. However in the early stage of transnational operation, BP's businesses were mainly distributed in Middle East (oil production) and Western Europe (petrochemical production), being less known in other regions especially America, the most attractive investment target country for all petroleum corporations in the world because of its locational advantages such as stable political environment, active private corporate culture, huge market size, and high-profit margin.

In 1958, BP intended to tap into the American market by cooperating with Sinclair Oil Corporation, which, however, did not achieve the desired results because oil export to America from other countries was put down since it issued the Mandatory Oil Import Quota Program at that time. Then in 1969, another opportunity for BP to invest in America emerged as huge petroleum reserve was discovered in Prudhoe Bay. To realize development in American market, BP must solve the following issues: (1) establish its own vertical network of petroleum production and operation; (2) acquire the market experiences and management ability required for conducting extensive business activities in America; (3) find solutions for responding to the energy market protection mechanism in America. BP decided to select a local enterprise in America as its partner. It targeted Standard Oil Company of Ohio because: (1) it occupied the largest fourth market share in America relying on its core business of petroleum refining and marketing; (2) it had strong management ability and financial strength to develop the market further; (3) its shareholding structure was decentralized, which would be easier for BP to acquire control over it; (4) it was lack of petroleum reserve. The ownership advantages of BP in upstream products were complementary with those of Standard Oil Company of Ohio in downstream products, which constituted the basis for their cooperation.

Case Analysis

This case describes the strategies taken by BP for tapping into the American market. The strategic thoughts and content have well embodied the basic characteristics of the globalization strategies of multinational corporations. We analyze the case in two aspects: strategic planning in early stage and strategic integration in later stage.

1. Strategic planning in early stage

In early 1970, BP acquired the initial shares of Standard Oil Company of Ohio by transferring most shares it held in Alaska oil field and partial downstream assets of Sinclair Oil Corporation. But the management of Standard Oil Company of Ohio was still independent from BP because the rights and interests of minority shareholders enjoyed more protection in US and it would be in contravention of the U.S. laws if BP interfered more with the operation of Standard Oil Company of Ohio. Besides, such independence helped avoid the punishment for non-compliance with the Sherman Act. Under the Sherman Act, every combination or conspiracy in restraint of trade or commerce is declared to be illegal, and if one party holds shares in another party to form affiliate relations, the two parties might conspire in the market behaviors such as pricing, which was in contradiction with the U.S. laws. The ownership advantages and locational advantages of BP were well reflected in this acquisition, while the internal advantages were not played effectively due to the restrictions in the cooperation agreement.

2. Strategic integration in later stage

The common interest of the two parties in the early stage after acquisition mainly lay in the oil exploitation in Prudhoe Bay. The huge oil reserve brought considerable profit for the two parties although the internal advantages of BP were not given full play. In 1970s, the position of Standard Oil Company of Ohio in the global market reached a high level and BP became more desirable to carry out necessary integration to incorporate Standard Oil Company of Ohio into its global planning as a controlled subsidiary. But Standard Oil Company of Ohio still maintained its independence because it believed that it would be detrimental to the legitimate rights and interest of minority shareholders and dissatisfy the existing employees if BP participated in the management of Standard Oil Company of Ohio as a major shareholder. In middle 1980s, America gradually released its control on oil imports, the strategic interest in American market became increasingly important for BP and Standard Oil Company of Ohio became the most important subsidiary of BP. Considering this, BP decided to acquire and integrate Standard Oil Company of Ohio further and replace its management members. Even though, BP still maintained the independence of Standard Oil Company of Ohio as it was required to protect the minority shareholders by the U.S. laws. Till 1987, BP acquired the remaining shares of Standard Oil Company of Ohio and obtained full control over it and subsequently, BP began to carry out effective integration to implement its global strategy with the internal advantages of its subsidiaries in and outside America.

Conclusion

The motive for international operation of BP is in line with the eclectic paradigm of international production. BP's further integration and acquisition of Standard Oil Company of Ohio were mainly for the purpose of benefit sharing, technology sharing and knowledge sharing and exploiting the internal advantages of BP to a higher extent, which played an important role in BP's global operation strategy and improved BP's position in the global energy market.

Questions

(1) What is the strategy of BP towards the American market? What is the core content of the strategy?

(2) What legal issues may be faced by BP in the development of strategic planning?

1.2　Wanda Group's Strategy for US Market

Related Knowledge

Enterprises Internationalization; Transnational M&A; Strategic objective;Strategy implementation

Case Description

On May 21, 2012, Wanda Group entered into a M&A agreement with American Multi-Cinema (AMC), the second largest movie theater chain across the world, under which Wanda Group acquired 100% shares of AMC with a consideration of $3.1 billion (including the total price of $2.6 billion for the shares acquired and the working capital up to $500 million to be invested in AMC after acquisition) and assumed the related liabilities of AMC.

Case Analysis

The case is mainly about Wanda Group's acquisition of AMC. It may be seen from the case that the strategic objectives of both Wanda Group and AMC are very clear.

1. Strategic objective of Wanda Group

Wanda Group started its investment in cultural industry by establishing Wanda movie theater chain in 2005 and formulated its ten-year strategic objective of international development in the cultural industry in 2010. The acquisition of AMC was one of its key initiatives towards this objective. Before acquisition, Wanda Group carried out detailed and comprehensive assessments and investigations on AMC, and it took this acquisition as the first step for its international deployment in the cultural industry. Once acquiring AMC, Wanda Group could expand its scope of business and take advantage of the resources and channels of AMC to cooperate with more well-known film companies. Besides, the acquisition could help Wanda Group tap into the U.S. market, which was a lot more bang for the buck. Most importantly, the acquisition enabled AMC and Wanda Group to share the film resources and capital flows to increase their financial income and realize stable growth of capital flows. In the long run, the acquisition of AMC helped Wanda Group mitigate the business risks it faced and improve its competitiveness in the U.S. market.

2. Strategic objective of AMC

Before the acquisition, AMC was in a great mess due to the economic crisis prevailing then and its poor management. At that time, the competition of movie theater chains in US intensified and the business performance of movie industry and box-office returns declined continuously. AMC suffered huge losses and debt. Its annual report showed that by the end of March 2012, the loss reached up to $82 million and the asset-liability ratio was as high as 96% (total assets of 3638 million and total liabilities of $3484 million). AMC faced tremendous difficulties to continue its operation and the major shareholders intended to dispose of it, which created a good opportunity for Wanda Group to acquire AMC.

Conclusion

The acquisition was a win-win strategy for Wanda Group and AMC. On the one hand, Wanda Group realized its strategic objective of internationalization through this acquisition, and on the other hand, AMC alleviated the dilemma it faced through such a wise strategic decision.

Questions

What's the strategy of Wanda Group for tapping into the U.S. market?

1.3   Strategic Layout of InBev in China

Related Knowledge

Transnational M&A; Transfer of shares; Strategic layout

Case Description

Sedrin Beer made a great progress from product-based operation to brand-based operation and finally to capital-based operation since 2001 by expansion of business scale and brand. Continuous economic development in China contributed to the improvement of people's life and brought great opportunities for the beer market in China. Numerous beer manufacturers in the world turned their eyes to China. At that point, Sedrin Beer planned to dispose of its shares. In order to attract more investors and obtain a higher offer, Sedrin Beer decided to sell both state-owned shares and non-state-owned shares together for the transferee to get absolute control over Sedrin Beer.

In mid-June 2005, Sedrin Beer engaged PWC as its financial adviser for the transfer of shares and in the end of July, it made the following decisions: (1) the shares of Sedrin Beer would be transferred in an on-exchange transaction mode under which the state-owned shares were listed for transfer in Fujian Property Right Transaction and the top 4 beer manufacturers in the world and top 3 beer manufacturers in China would be invited as the bidders; (2) two rounds of bidding were organized, that is, selection of qualified bidders in the first round, bidding and award in the second round; (3) the transferee was required to keep the place of registration, tax payment place, brand, and management and employees of Sedrin Beer unchanged after the transfer.

The second round of bidding was conducted on December 7, 2005 in Fujian Property Right Transaction, and finally only one bidder named InBev from Belgium submitted the bid and finally acquired Sedrin Beer at a price of RMB 5.886 billion.

On January 23, 2006, the headquarters of InBev in Belgium announced officially that it would acquire 100% shares of Sedrin Beer at a total price of RMB 5.886 billion and in two stages, namely 39.48% state-owned shares at a price of RMB 2.324 billion in the first stage, and then the remaining 60.52% non-state-owned shares at a price of RMB 3.562 billion by the end of 2007. In the following one month, InBev and Sedrin Beer finalized the specific terms of transfer of shares through negotiation and finally executed a total of 25 acquisition agreements including the three most important ones "Share Transfer Agreement" "Agreement on Maintaining Tax Payment Place Unchanged" "Commitment on Not to Carrying out Structural Layoff ".

Case Analysis

The case describes the process of InBev's acquisition of Sedrin Beer in which a positive-sum game benefited all parties involved.

1. For Sedrin Beer

(1) Appreciation of shares. Sedrin Beer was sold at a price of RMB 5.886 billion against the net assets of just RMB 600 million, achieving a premium rate as high as 1000%; (2) Sedrin Beer achieved sustainable development and protected its brand. Under the agreements between the two parties, InBev was required to hold the shares of Sedrin Beer for a long term and take advantage of its resources to improve Sedrin Beer's international position, it was not allowed to limit the development and brand expansion of Sedrin Beer; (3) the management and employees of Sedrin Beer were retained. Within the specified period of time after the transfer, InBev may not conduct structural layoff or replace the management team of Sedrin Beer, and must adopt an incentive mechanism in line with the international practices.

2. For local government

Benefits for Putian city in Fujian province, where Sedrin Beer is located: (1) the transfer of shares of Sedrin Beer contributed financial revenue of RMB 800 million to the local government; (2) maximum social benefits were realized. The place of registration, tax payment place and brand of Sedrin Beer were unchanged after the transfer. Sedrin Beer could continue to make contribution to the financial revenue of Putian and help improve the international awareness of Sedrin Beer and Putian.

3. For InBev

The Vice President of InBev who was in charge of the legal and corporate affairs in Asia Pacific stated that it was a value-added transaction for InBev to acquire Sedrin Beer, and it was also a necessary step for InBev's strategic layout and market expansion.

Conclusion

The continuing openness policy of China brought more and more favorable investment opportunities for foreign investors. InBev's acquisition of Sedrin Beer was a successful case and also a wise strategic decision of InBev for realizing scale economy and global deployment.

Questions

Which characteristics of multinational corporations are reflected in the strategic layout of InBev in China?

1.4   Apple's Strategy in China

Related Knowledge

Multinational corporations; Global strategy; Localization strategy; Strategy choices

Case Description

Apple, formerly known as Apple Computer Inc. before 2017, is one of the largest IT companies and the No.1 mobile phone manufacturer in the world. There is no doubt that Apple is the leader among the successful IT product manufacturers across the globe. Why are iPhones so popular? The reason also lies in its business strategy in addition to the outstanding appearance, quality, and performance of its products.

Case Analysis

This case mainly describes the business strategies of Apple Inc., of which both the advantages and the disadvantages should be analyzed based on the strategy theory.

1. Advantages of Apple

(1) iPhones are designed with special workmanship to offer graceful appearance, good experience and user-friendly operation for the consumers, which are obviously different

from other phones in the market. In addition, iPhones use the unique iOS system which enables high usability and convenience and allows for easy development, upgrade and repair. Moreover, Apple Inc. makes innovations constantly to develop new products adapted to the demands of consumers and then attract more and more users.

(2) Apple has been named the world's most valuable brand by *Forbes* magazine for several consecutive years. Especially in 2019, Apple's worth topped $205.5 billion, up 12 percent over the previous year, which is the first company to cross the $200 billion threshold. The value of brand decides the prospect of an enterprise. Every enterprise has its own development mode. In a long run, the mode of Apple is impossible to be copied or substituted.

(3) As the only IT giant that manufactures both hardware and software, Apple attaches great importance to the research and development of advanced technologies and has established powerful R&D centers. From the 1st to the 10th generation products, iPhones are always designed with the most advanced and unique technologies then, e.g. touch screen, multi-touch, Retina screen, front camera, video call, back glass, wireless charging and facial recognition. Relying on the excellent design, Apple products are always leading revolutionary changes in a certain aspect in the market and have become the model of other competitors.

2. Disadvantages of Apple

(1) iPhones are designed as high-end products, which are not affordable for some consumers because of increasingly high prices and limited options. The price of one iPhone is almost equivalent to a pretty good laptop. In such case, the consumers may prefer other brands.

(2) Some key parts of iPhones are often in short supply. The competitiveness of Apple would decline when it could not meet the changing demands in the market. For example, Apple has only a few suppliers of computer displays. Once the products provided by the suppliers are defective, it is hard to find substitute suppliers because of the stringent technical requirements of Apple, which might lead to delivery delays.

(3) Although iPhones are very popular in China, the after-sale services are unsatisfactory. According to the statistics of the China Consumer Association in 2012, the complaints about after-sale services accounted for 25.6% of the total consumer complaints about iPhones.

Conclusion

The success of Apple depends on its technological strength and strategies in operation and management. As a multinational enterprise, Apple's business strategy for Chinese market should focus on how to give full play to its product advantages, brand advantages and R&D strength, and optimize its pricing strategy, supply chain, and after-sales services to meet the demands of consumers constantly.

Questions

In the overseas operation, what could the Chinese enterprises learn from the strategy of Apple for Chinese market?

Chapter 2

Social Responsibility of Multinational Corporations

2.1 Google's Monopoly in EU Market

Related Knowledge

Multinational corporations; Market monopolies; Market dominance; Abuse of market dominance

Case Description

In June 2017, the European Commission fined Google 2.42 billion euros for abusing its dominance as a search engine by giving an illegal advantage to its comparison shopping service, which was subject to the antitrust laws. In November 2021, European General Court affirmed the decision.

The comparison shopping service is one of Google's specialized search services that get product offers from merchant websites based on user searches, allowing users to compare prices of merchants that can be listed without making payments. In addition, search results may also show online search ads placed by Google AdWords, and AdWords search results can be purchased by any advertiser.

Case Analysis

This case mainly involves Google's monopoly in the EU market. According to the applicable EU regulations on market operation, the EU determines the abuse of market dominance and behavior of monopoly of enterprises mainly based on the following considerations.

1. Possessing a dominant market position

An important factor in defining market dominance is the large market share held by an enterprise. The European Commission found that since 2008, Google's search engine had held more than 90% of the market share in EEA countries, while one of its main competitors, Bing, held just less than 5%. According to the precedents of the Court of Justice of the European Union (CJEU), a dominant market position can be established when an enterprise has a market share of 70%-80%. Thus, Google is presumed to have a dominant position in the search engine market. The fact that the service is provided free of charge is a factor considered in assessment of dominance.

2. Behavior of abusing market dominance

Google highlights its own comparison shopping service on its general search results page. Although competing comparison shopping services can only be displayed as general search results and are able to lower the ranking of web pages on search results pages with the aid of certain algorithms, Google gives its own comparison shopping services preferential treatment by highlighting them and setting them up algorithmically so that they would never be lowered in ranking due to other websites' algorithms. This is a typical example of abusing market dominance, crowding out competitors and disrupting the order of market competition.

3. Behavior in digital economy

In the case of Google's monopoly, although market share is the main factor based on which the European Commission concluded that Google had market dominance, when determining Google's abuse of market dominance, the European Commission not only considered the influence of network externalities on formation of a market barrier, but also analyzed Google's manipulation of its algorithm to placing its own comparison shopping sites at the top of search results.

Conclusion

The digital economy poses challenges to the determination of abuse of market dominance, especially in the following three aspects: (1) the difficulty of defining the underlying market; (2) the complexity of the abuse of market dominance; (3) the concealment of the abuse of market dominance. Therefore in the era of digital economy, it is critical to fully recognize the characteristics of the digital economy, and then to analyze the antitrust regulations and rules based on the characteristics of the Internet industry to keep pace with the times, so as to achieve the purpose of protecting market competition.

Questions

Please try to explain how a host country should regulate the behavior of monopoly of multinational corporations, with reference to the content of international business law concerning international investment.

2.2   Product Liabilities in Takata Airbag

Related Knowledge

Multinational corporations; Product liability; Protection of consumer rights and interests

Case Description

Founded in 1933 and headquartered in Tokyo, Japan, Takata is a multinational corporation specializing in the production of auto airbags, steering wheels, seat belts, electronic sensing devices and other auto safety components. Takata provided airbags for Toyota, Mitsubishi, BMW and many other automakers. At its peak, it gained 22% of the global airbag market and was one of the three largest airbag makers in the world at that time.

On May 16, 2009, an 18-year-old girl in the United States drove a Honda Accord made in 2000 and collided with another car. After the airbag was deployed, the girl had her carotid artery lacerated by the metal fragment shooting from the airbag, and eventually the girl bled to death. Subsequently, the issue of Takata's airbag defect came into public view.

At least 23 people were killed and hundreds injured worldwide due to safety incidents caused by Takata airbags by 2019. According to data released by the media, as of May 2017, the total number of defective autos recalled around the world due to defective airbags was as high as 120 million, involving 19 auto brands, almost all mainstream auto brands such as Mercedes-Benz, BMW, Ford, Volkswagen, GM, Toyota, Nissan and Tesla. In 2017, the automakers that cooperated with Takata recalled the defective autos and implemented the corresponding compensation schemes, and meanwhile made claim of a huge amount against Takata. In these cases, apart from the high liquidated damages, Takata had to pay compensation for personal injury. Takata's financial report of 2016 showed that Takata had sales of 662.5 billion yen and a loss of up to 79.5 billion yen. Additionally, Takata had to pay 850 million dollars to the world's major automakers. On June 26, 2017, Takata filed for bankruptcy protection with the Tokyo District Court, while its core subsidiary in the United States "TK Holdings" also filed for bankruptcy protection with the local court. In 2018, the total number of vehicles recalled by China due to "Takata airbag" problem exceeded 1.7 million, accounting for 14.19% of the total number of autos recalled that year. Starting in 2019, a number of automakers, including Subaru, Tesla, BMW, Volkswagen, Daimler truck, Mercedes-Benz and Ferrari, launched a new round of recall because of Takata airbags with potential safety hazards.

Case Analysis

This case mainly describes the defect of auto airbags produced by Takata and its serious effects and consequences.

Takada's auto airbags have serious defect. Takada installed gas propellants in its airbags which were designed to allow the airbags to deploy more quickly in the event of auto crashes. However, the propellant is filled in a piece of metal, which will automatically eject in the event of auto collision. In order to reduce the cost, Takata used ammonium nitrate in the gas generator. This material will deteriorate and be affected with moisture when not properly stored, which can easily cause the inflatable generator to explode, and the fragments shooting during the explosion will pose a safety threat to the front passengers. In nearly ten years, Takata airbags caused many irreparable accidents, resulting in more than 20 deaths and hundreds of injuries. Consumers not only suffered personal injury, but also had to spend a lot of money on follow-up repair, buy new auto airbags or even new cars, and sometimes pay huge medical bills. The death caused by Takata's airbags has brought long-term pain to the families who have lost their loved ones. Takada, as the culprit, not only had to pay a huge sum of compensation to the auto companies that cooperated with it, but also had to compensate the families of the consumers involved in the accidents, with the compensation amounting to several billion yuan. In the end, Takata and its U.S. subsidiary were declared bankrupt in 2017 because they could not afford such high amount of compensation.

Auto safety is very important. The safety system of autos mainly includes airbags and seat belts. Previously, according to the findings of the National Highway Traffic Safety Administration, proper use of airbags can reduce driver fatalities by 11% and frontal impact force by 30%. It can be said that in the event of vehicle collision during driving, the airbag can reduce the injury degree of the occupants and protect the life safety of the occupants to the greatest extent.

As a multinational corporation, Takata was once one of the world's three largest airbag manufacturers with one-fifth of the global airbag market share. It had a subsidiary in the United States and cooperated with many well-known auto brands. Such wretched incident happening to Takata involved many well-known auto brands, causing certain negative impacts on their reputation, and bringing irreparable damage to automakers and consumers. It is clear that automakers should put more effort and invest financial resources to improve the quality of products. Otherwise, fatal accidents would happen once such incident arises.

Nowadays, global auto production is achieved through global procurement, such as purchase of airbags made in Japan and tires made in German, because this mode can significantly reduce costs, thus enabling enterprises to earning more profits. However, problems arising from it are obvious. Of course, procurement from a single company also has disadvantages, as procurement of auto parts from a single company can cause the company's monopoly on the auto parts market, while other competing companies get into difficulties. If too much reliance is placed on a single company to source auto parts, then once the company is unable to deliver the products, the auto seller must adjust the schedule of its parts supply. Additionally, if a large number of auto parts are purchased from a single company, the company may reduce costs in order to make more money, thereby resulting in lower quality and more serious risks. This is because the problems arising from product liability are usually serious, persistent and potentially dangerous.

The Takata airbag incident began in 2009. Until 2019, millions of autos were still recalled every year due to the Takata airbag problem. Potential dangers still existed, drivers had to face the dangers on the road and carefully check the auto parts when driving. Therefore, automakers should learn from the Takata airbag incident, face the problems squarely and improve the technology so as to remain invincible in the fierce market competition.

Conclusion

The Takata airbag incident in Japan has aroused the public's concern about auto safety and undermined consumers' trust in the products of some multinational corporations. Although Takata went bankrupt, the incident left a profound lesson. According to the product liability laws and implementation rules of most countries, when a defective product causes property damage or personal injury to consumers, users or third parties of the product, the manufacturer or seller of the product shall be jointly liable for compensation.

Questions

Try to compare the definition of product liability in common law and civil law systems.

2.3   Valspar Coating Pollution Incident

Related Knowledge

Multinational corporations; Environmental pollution; Corporate social responsibility

Case Description

On July 17, 2018, Jiading District Bureau of Environment Protection in Shanghai made an administrative penalty of RMB 100,000 on Valspar Coatings (Shanghai) Co., Ltd. for environmental non-compliance (failure to install pollution prevention and control facilities for and fugitive emission of waste gas containing volatile organic compounds) with Article 45 and Item 1, Paragraph 1 of Article 108 of the Law of the People's Republic of China on the Prevention and Control of Atmospheric Pollution.

Valspar Coatings (Shanghai) Co., Ltd. had ever been punished for several times previously. On December 20, 2016, it was fined RMB 120,000 by Jiading District Bureau of Environment Protection for violation of Article 45 of the Law of the People's Republic of China on the Prevention and Control of Atmospheric Pollution, and ordered to immediately make corrections. The reason for punishment was "the production activities generating waste gas containing volatile organic compounds was not conducted in an enclosed space or equipment". Later on January 10, 2017, it was fined and ordered to make correction of illegal act by Jiading District Bureau of Environment Protection in Shanghai for violation against the management regulations on the prevention and control of pollution. On April 26, 2018, it was fined RMB 70,000 by Jiading District Bureau of Environment Protection in Shanghai for "failure to install pollution prevention and control facilities for and fugitive emission of waste gas containing volatile organic compounds". On July 2, 2019, it was fined RMB 70,000 by Jiading District Bureau of Ecology and Environment for "fugitive emission of waste gas".

Case Analysis

This case mainly describes the fact that Valspar Coatings (Shanghai) Co., Ltd. was imposed administrative penalties by the environmental authorities of Jiading District, Shanghai for repeated violations of China's environmental protection law during production.

Valspar Corporation is the sixth largest manufacturer of paints and coatings, a business it has engaged in since 1806. Having operations in 26 countries across the world, Valspar is the global leader in coatings on coil steel surfaces and also the leader in China's furniture coatings market.

Valspar Coatings (Shanghai) Co., Ltd. was founded on October 20, 1999, with a registered capital of 15.1 million dollars. Its shareholder is Valspar (Asia) Co., Ltd. It is mainly engaged in the production of coatings, paints, mixed solvents and mixed additives, selling its own products and providing after-sales services and technical guidance for its products.

As a multinational corporation, Valspar Coatings (Shanghai) Co., Ltd. was fined by Jiading District Bureau of Ecology and Environment many times for its violation of Articles 45 and 108 of the Law of the People's Republic of China on the Prevention and Control of Atmospheric Pollution. But it still failed to make rectification despite of repeated punishments, showing a serious lack of corporate social responsibility. In developed countries, due to the strict pollutants emission standards, the penalties for discharge or emission beyond the limits are relatively heavy. In order to avoid hefty fines, enterprises tend to strictly comply with the pollution discharge regulations. Therefore, some multinational corporations strictly follow the green production standards to control the pollution level in their home countries, but in China they disregard their responsibilities for environmental protection and reduce the cost in order to maximize their own interests, thus exacerbating the environmental pollution problem in China.

Recent years witness the volume and amount of investments made by multinational corporations in China have continued to increase. In 2018 alone, the foreign capital utilized by China amounted to RMB 885.61 billion, making it the second largest recipient of foreign capital inflow in the world. The establishment of a large number of foreign-funded enterprises, along with China's previous imperfect environmental protection management systems has brought severe environmental pollution problems to China. Although the growth rate of China's foreign investment has slowed down in recent years, the environmental pollution caused by it should not be underestimated. From the perspective of the types of multinational corporations, most of the multinational corporations investing in China are mainly processing and manufacturing enterprises, accounting for two-thirds of all multinational corporations, and those engaging in resource development and service provision rank behind them. From the perspective of industry structure, most of the cross-border direct investments received by China are in the manufacturing industry which produces the most pollutants (especially waste gas pollutants) and many manufacturing industries are pollution-intensive. These pollution-intensive industries mainly refer to those enterprises that will directly or indirectly produce a large number of pollutants in the production process if they are not controlled. These pollutants may cause serious damage to life and health of humans, animals and plants, deteriorate the environment and affect the ecological quality.

Conclusion

China should adhere to the development of a green economy, step up government oversight, improve applicable laws and systems, strengthen supervision and inspection by law enforcement departments, and ensure that any enterprise that discharges pollutants in violation of laws and regulations must be held liable and law enforcement is strict, fair and reasonable. Meanwhile, it is important to establish a strict environmental protection audit system for access of foreign-funded enterprises, strictly implement the access criteria, establish and improve the incentive mechanism for multinational corporations to fulfill their corporate social responsibilities in China, encourage multinational corporations to take active measures to assume their corporate responsibilities in China, and implement the measures for proper rewards and punishments.

Questions

Please try to explain the practical significance of multinational corporations to fulfill their social responsibilities, with reference to the incident of Valspar coating pollution.

2.4   False Advertising of Canada Goose

Related Knowledge

Foreign-owned enterprises; Marketing; False advertising; Unfair competition

Case Description

Xiji Shanghai Trade Company Ltd., an affiliate of Canada Goose, was fined RMB450,000 by Shanghai Municipal Administration for Maket Regulation for deceiving and misleading consumers by making false claims in advertisements.

The Canada Goose down garments that cost tens of thousands of RMB at every turn and were attractive on social media became a complete flop for its false advertisement claiming that "all of our down materials contain the excellent and warmest Canadian goose down ...". In fact, most of the down garments sold by it were not made of highly fluffy goose down with better thermal insulation performance, but made of duck down with lower fill power. Therefore, its claim that the down used in its products is "excellent and warmest" is false.

Given the webpage clicks of Canada Goose's Tmall flagship store hit 181 million and the sales reached RMB167 million in 2020, the advertisement involved in the case is expected to have some social impact. In accordance with the relevant provisions of the Advertising Law of the People's Republic of China, the market regulator decided to impose a fine of RMB450,000 on Xiji Shanghai Trade Company Ltd., and order it to stop publishing illicit advertisements and eliminate the influence within the corresponding scope.

Case Analysis

This is a case in which a foreign-owned enterprise in China misled the consumers and damaged the rights and interests of consumers mainly by making false claims in advertisements to seek improper benefits.

Foreign-invested enterprises are often praised highly for their superiority of imported goods, and the prices of their products are often sky-high. In order to attract Chinese consumers, Canada Goose even hyped the warmth retention of its down garments, using absolute words such as warmest. Moreover, it used inferior duck down as substitute for high-quality goose down, which constituted false claims in advertisement and violated the Advertising Law of the People's Republic of China.

The Advertising Law of the People's Republic of China prohibits absolute words such as highest level and best in advertising. Canada Goose's false claims in advertisement focusing on the warmth valued by the consumers have misled the consumers and constituted unfair competition against similar products on the market. Such acts were illegal.

Conclusion

Compliance with laws is the legal bottom line that an enterprise should maintain. Either Chinese enterprises or foreign-invested enterprises, once they enter a market, should be responsible to the consumers in the market and prohibited from using illegal means to deceive consumers and crowding out competitors in the industry in exchange for huge profits.

Questions

Please try to explain how a host country should effectively control unfair competition behaviors of multinational corporations with reference to the above case.

2.5 Google's Tax Avoidance Arouses Public Concern

Related Knowledge

Multinational corporations; International tax evasion; International tax avoidance; International taxation jurisdiction

Case Description

As one of the world's leading multinational corporations, Google has its own management organizations and branches in many countries and regions around the world. In July 2017, the French tax authority accused Google of using tax loopholes to evade the taxes of 1.12 billion euros it should have paid in a Paris court. The French government held that Google earned a large amount of revenue from France but paid only the lowest corporate tax in France. Google transferred its income generated in French to Ireland to avoid paying French corporate taxes. However, this case ended with Google's winning.

The Times of the United Kingdom reported in 2009 that Google earned a profit of 1.6 billion pounds from its advertisements placed in the United Kingdom in 2008, but did not pay taxes. In November 2009, Turkish tax authority fined Google 71 million liras and vigorously denounced Google's tax avoidance.

Case Analysis

This case mainly describes the fact and act of Google's international tax avoidance. As a technology giant with the world's largest search engine, Google generates considerable revenue each year, which is taxable.

According to the U.S. tax law, U.S. companies are required to pay 25%-35% tax on their overseas profits, while relevant data show that Google paid only 2.4% tax on its non-US income per year. On the one hand, Google took advantage of tax havens to reduce the tax burden. Google registered different offshore companies as subsidiaries, concentrating their spending in areas with high tax rates and their revenues in Bermuda, a "tax haven" with very low tax rates. On the other hand, as intangible assets are non-substantive, non-comparable in value and uncertain in revenue, the use of transfer pricing of intangible assets for tax avoidance is more concealed and not easily detected by tax authorities. Google has cleverly used this feature to effectively avoid taxes by selling the right to use its intellectual property.

Google has adopted the double Irish with a Dutch sandwich model, namely Google Ireland

Holdings-the Netherlands-Google Ireland. First, Google Ireland Holdings is a holding subsidiary of Google in Bermuda which purchases the intellectual property rights developed by Google in the United States and the royalties in Europe, Africa and the Middle East, and then transfers them to Google Ireland. Google could skillfully avoid taxes in Ireland as what was collected in the process of transfer was fee of licensing intellectual property. Google Ireland, the Dublin business unit of Google Ireland Holdings, is also the ultimate owner of the right to use intangible assets. It mainly sold Google's web ads to the world and generated profits accounting for 88% of its total overseas profits. The company eventually transferred the revenues to Google Ireland Holdings in Bermuda in the form of paying royalties on intellectual property rights. As Google is not a company based in a member state of the EU and cannot enjoy preferential tax treatment in Ireland, in order to avoid taxes in Ireland, Google Ireland used shell firms without employees in the Netherlands by first paying to such shell firms and then transferring about 99.8% of the royalties from such shell firms to Bermuda. Although the process was complicated, it increased Google's profit by about 26% and saved nearly 3.1 billion dollars in tax expenses.

Although Google won the lawsuit in the tax avoidance case in France, some countries were dissatisfied with its acts of tax avoidance. Earlier, Italian tax authority accused Google of evading about 306 million euros from 2009 to 2013, all of which was transferred to Ireland by Google. Subsequently, Google decided to settle the tax dispute with Italy and pay the overdue taxes to the Italian government. In 2016, EU introduced new regulations to crack down on tax avoidance by multinational corporations, requiring large multinational corporations with annual revenues of over 750 million euros and registered within EU to report annually to the EU their business incomes in each member state of EU and the tax payment to other countries in that year.

Conclusion

The international tax law systems are very complicated in practice, which involve not only the subject and object of international tax laws, but also the basic relationship of international taxation. As multinational taxpayers, multinational corporations must comply with the relevant laws and regulations of the host countries, otherwise they will bear the corresponding legal consequences. With the development of cooperation in international taxation, there will be increasingly less room for international tax avoidance and evasion by multinational corporations.

Questions

Please try to understand the practical significance of cracking down on international tax evasion and international tax avoidance with reference to Google's case of tax avoidance.

Chapter 3

Transnational Direct Investment

3.1 Greenfield Investment of Orient International

Related Knowledge

Transnational direct investment; Greenfield investment; Investment environment; Legal environment

Case Description

On September 22, 2020, Orient International commenced its Sweater Manufacturing Base Phase I Project in Ethiopia, which was the first greenfield investment of Orient International under the Belt and Road Initiative and the Go out strategy and representing the "biggest order" so far.

The project was located in Phase II of Addis Ababa National Industrial Park of Ethiopia, and it was planned to build three sweater manufacturing workshops with the total floor area of 62,000 m^2 and the total investment of RMB 300 million. The workshops could accommodate 1,200 computerized flat knitting machines and 2,000 sewing machines. The proposed project duration was one year and once completed, the manufacturing base could realize a production capacity of 10 million sweaters per year. This project was a key initiative for Orient International to build its core capabilities of sweater manufacturing and extend to European and American markets to realize global deployment. Although the outbreak of COVID-19 pandemic brought the global economy to a near-standstill and impeded the outbound investment projects of Chinese enterprises, the project team of Orient International made a success that seemed "impossible" during the COVID-19 pandemic period.

Case Analysis

As the largest foreign trade enterprise in Shanghai, Orient International always responds actively to the national initiative and strategy to move forward step by step in the way of international production capacity cooperation.

To implement the globalization strategy, Oriental International deployed its production and manufacturing, trade and sales, technology research and development, and supply chain logistics businesses across the globe and carried out widespread economic and trade investment cooperation. It built factories in several countries along the Belt and Road to realize a transformation from "made in China" to "made overseas". In order to expand its footprint overseas, Orient International made in-depth investigations and research on several African countries including Ethiopia, Côte d'Ivoire, and Burkina Faso. By following the economic rules of international production capacity cooperation and transfer, it could take advantage of the preferential policies, labor and raw materials locally to realize overseas expansion.

Facing the worldwide COVID-19 pandemic, Orient International selected a positive and steady investment strategy to protect its investment and construction projects in Africa. To ensure the commencement of the project as scheduled on September 22, 2020, Orient International sent a project team consisting of 7 members to Ethiopia in August 2020, when it was in the toughest time of the pandemic. Under their joint efforts for nearly one hundred days to overcome the difficulties like short supply of containers, rise of sea freight and main materials prices, the project team completed the construction of foundations of all the three workshops and the installation and acceptance inspection of the main steel structure (beam, column, purlin, and floor bearing plate) of the first workshop on December 31, 2020. The logistics team in China also completed the shipment of steel structures and other materials (275 containers in total) to ensure the uninterrupted construction on site. In the end February 2021, all sections of the project on site passed the quality acceptance inspection at one time and the project was completed nearly one month ahead of the planned completion date.

Orient International promoted international cultural exchanges. President Xi Jinping has ever mentioned the importance of the development of young talents in Africa in 2018 Beijing Summit of the Forum on China-Africa Cooperation by stating that the young in Africa needed more occupational training opportunities and jobs and space of development. In response, Orient International deployed extensive education and training resources in Africa to give full play of the fundamental, guiding, and supportive basic role of education. In recent years, Orient International established multiple education and training facilities in Africa, e.g. the Belt and Road for Textile Industry education and training base in Addis Ababa, founded jointly with Donghua University in September 2018. Besides, the "Oriental Fashion Development Department" under Orient International entered into a memorandum of understanding with the Unioncamere of Italy for cooperation on several events like Shanghai Fashion Week to realize sharing of resources and mutual complementarity. All of these laid solid foundation for the profound and extensive development of Orient International in the fashion industry.

It is shown from this case that before deciding to make a greenfield investment, the investor needs to analyze its own strategy and the investment environment of the host country to evaluate whether the investment would help improve its competitiveness. Greenfield investment in less developed regions means relatively low access threshold and a dominant position in the competition with local enterprises. But it also needs a huge amount of money and time for establishing a new marketing network and obtaining the cultural identity of stakeholders and external legitimacy to a certain extent.

Conclusion

Greenfield investment involves significant risks due to long construction duration and capital investment and the investor might face great difficulties with cultural differences, government regulation, exclusion of local enterprises, and internal organization and management at the initial stage. The success of Orient International in greenfield investment is useful for other Chinese enterprises interested in transnational direct investment.

Questions

(1) Evaluate the legal environment of the transnational investment of Orient International;

(2) Which legal issues may be involved in the host country about the greenfield investment of transnational direct investment?

3.2　A Successful Acquisition Made by SANY

Related Knowledge

Transnational direct investment; Transnational M & A; Cultural integration

Case Description

As compared with the great potential in overseas market, the enterprises in the construction machinery industry in China face increasing pressure in recent years as the domestic market saturates. Before transnational acquisition, SANY took the domestic market as its primary target and the revenue from overseas market just accounted for 10%. After extension to the overseas market, SANY welcomed a great change.

Putzmeister, a Germany company intended to sell its shares because it suffered heavy losses in the widespread financial crisis in 2008 and being a family firm, the successors of the founder were unwilling to operate the company as a going concern. Therefore, Putzmeister visited SANY on December 20, 2011 and issued an offer for sale. In early January 2012,

SANY sent a reply letter to Putzmeister which stated its intent of acquisition and later the two parties agreed on a preliminary intention of acquisition. On January 31, 2012, SANY announced to the public that it acquired 90% shares of Putzmeister jointly with CITIC Industrial Investment Fund at a price of 360 million euros. And on July 1, 2013, SANY acquired the remaining 10% shares of Putzmeister to obtain 100% control.

Case Analysis

This case mainly describes the process of SANY's acquisition of Putzmeister. SANY is the leader of the construction machinery industry in China. Both SANY and Putzmeister achieved further development after the acquisition transaction.

In terms of production cost, SANY acquired the leading technology of Putzmeister which would help mitigate its risks in innovation, reduce the production cost, and consolidate its position in the industry chain, while Putzmeister could take advantage of the low labor cost in China to reduce overall production cost and improve profitability.

In terms of market share, although Putzmeister took high market share in developed countries as a world-renowned brand with production facilities established all over the world and sales and service branches set up in more than 100 countries, it did not achieve the desired operating results in the Chinese market because of its "high quality and high pricing" based marketing mode. The acquisition helped Putzmeister reduce the production cost, and improve its market share in China. Similarly, SANY also improved its market share significantly after this acquisition.

In terms of global deployment, Putzmeister's brand image helped SANY extend its route of international development and accelerate the pace of integration with the European and American markets. Moreover, SANY could learn the internationally leading management ideas and methods from Putzmeister to upgrade its international business level.

Putzmeister has relatively well-established corporate culture and internationally recognized brand image as the leader in the construction machinery industry of German. In order to protect the brand value and maximize the effects of acquisition and integration, it was necessary to maintain the brand independence of Putzmeister. Therefore SANY adopted the "segregation before integration" strategy after acquisition. Such strategy mitigated greatly the cost and risk of cultural integration and maintained the autonomy and independence of Putzmeister. The two enterprises kept their operation independently of each other to a certain extent, and also learnt from and gave support to each other to realize the ultimate goal of win-win.

Conclusion

Transnational acquisition is an important means for internationalization of enterprises. The enterprises interested in transnational acquisition should accurately assess the production cost and market share before and after the acquisition and attach importance to the brand value of both parties. The cultural factors, cultural risks and cultural integration should also be valued in internationalization.

Questions

(1) What experience can be referenced from SANY's acquisition of Putzmeister?

(2) What's the difference between acquisition and greenfield investment in transnational direct investment?

3.3   Lessons from the Merger of BenQ and Siemens

Related Knowledge

Transnational direct investment; Transnational M&A; Cultural conflict; Cultural integration

Case Description

BenQ was desirous of building its own brand since it became the largest mobile phone OEM in 2005. For achieving this goal, the best choice was to merge with a well-known international brand. Then it found an opportunity when the negotiation between Siemens and Motorola failed. On June 8, 2005, BenQ announced officially that it acquired the mobile phone business of Siemens. It seemed a very budget-friendly deal then because BenQ did not pay any consideration, but won the lucrative dowry of 250 million euros from Siemens and was granted the essential patented technologies of Siemens in the fields of GSM, GPRS and 3G. But the deal also brought great burden to BenQ because Siemens' mobile phone business was in huge loss.

Case Analysis

This is an unsuccessful case of a Chinese corporation acquiring a foreign corporation. Although BenQ was well prepared for taking over the mobile phone business of Siemens before the merger, the two corporations were not well integrated with each other as expected, especially in cultural integration.

The corporate system and the social system of the two corporations vary too greatly to be integrated. Siemens is a "professionalism-oriented" organization while BenQ is a "pioneering spirit" oriented one. Siemens is deeply rooted in its corporate culture as a well-known large-scale enterprise in Europe, which is hard to be absorbed or changed by such an emerging Chinese enterprise as BenQ. From the perspective of product strategy, Siemens focuses on high-quality and high-end products and innovation, while BenQ pays more attention to product design and customer needs as a traditional OEM. From the perspective of management, BenQ is an entrepreneurial organization that emphasizes novelty and speed, while Siemens is a management organization that is more focused on processes and procedures. And with respect to the operation, Siemens values the integrity of procedures and regulations, while BenQ prefers to flexibility. One pursues high-speed, high-flexibility, and opportunism, and the other pursues prudency, compliance, and perfectionism, each with its distinct features.

Adequate study on the culture of the acquisition target was not carried out. Prior to entering into the acquisition agreement, it is necessary for the acquirer to establish a due diligence team to conduct an investigation and analysis on the national culture, enterprise history, development strategy, and other in-depth issues of the acquisition target in a reasonable, systemic, and scientific manner and compare the corporate cultures of the two. Where the cultures of the two parties are too distinct to achieve integration, the acquisition is meaningless.

BenQ was also influenced by the political, cultural and legal factors in the process of integration with Siemens, and such direct risks from culture and institution conflicts increased the cost of integration. For example, as banned by the strict protection mechanism for local workers and obstructed by the local organizations in German, BenQ was not allowed to lower the salary level of Germany employees or carry out layoffs.

Corporate strategy was not well integrated with the corporate culture. The integration of corporate strategy with corporate culture is a dynamic process in which the employees must be involved in and recognize the changes. Integration just for cultural purpose is unwise, which will incur additional cost of integration and lead to conflict. As for enterprise development, there is no way to tell which culture is better or superior. It is the best only when it is fit for the strategic development of the enterprise. The corporate culture will contribute to the sustainable development of an enterprise only when it is well integrated with the corporate strategy.

Conclusion

The merger of BenQ and the mobile phone division of Siemens is a representative case in the transnational M&A of Chinese enterprises which failed at last. It may be concluded from the cause analysis on the case that before initializing the M&A, the intending party must carry out comprehensive assessment and preparations and cultural evaluation on the target and the country where it is located, and after the M&A, conduct strategic integration and cultural integration with the target in a well-organized way.

Questions

Make a summary of the lessons from the case of BenQ & Siemens merger, based on the related content of transnational direct investment.

3.4   Transnational Investment under the Belt and Road Initiative

Related Knowledge

Transnational direct investment; Transnational M&A; Transfer of shares and legal regulation

Case Description

Israel is famous for its high-yield cows and advanced milk production technologies. Tnuva is one of the largest comprehensive food producers in Israel that has run for over 80 years and occupies a market share of more than 50% in the milk products industry in Israel, relying on its world's leading level in milk products research and development, animal husbandry and management. The shares of Tnuva are held by Apax Partner (56.7%), a British private equity investment company, Mivtach Shamir (21%), an Israeli investment company, and the local collective communities and agricultural cooperatives (22.3%).

Bright Food Group began to engage with Tnuva in September 2013 when the major shareholder Apax Partner was just planning for the listing of Tnuva. Upon receiving the intent of Bright Food, Apax Partner decided to abandon listing and negotiate with Bright Food for cooperation, while another shareholder Mivtach Shamir who enjoyed tag along rights decided to retain its shares to cooperate with Bright Food. On May 22, 2014, Bright Food and Apax Partner reached a preliminary acquisition agreement on the transfer of shares of Tnuva.

In August 2014, the application of Bright Food for acquisition of 56% shares of Tnuva was approved by the Ministry of Commerce of China. The shares would be jointly transferred to Bright Food and a Chinese financial institution with the shareholding of 36% and 20% respectively. However, just prior to the agreed closing date in January 2015, the minority shareholder Mivtach Shamir proposed to exercise its tag along right to sell its shares together with the major shareholder. If Bright Food required Mivtach Shamir to retain its shares, Bright Food had to accept other commercial conditions and if the closing could not be completed as agreed, Bright Food would pay high liquidated damages. In such a case, Bright Food had only two options: purchasing the shares of Mivtach Shamir by paying additional consideration, which was subject to further approval of the Ministry of Commerce (generally taking around three months); or seeking another partner or requesting the original partner to pay additional consideration. Unfortunately, the original partner decided to terminate the cooperation and not to participate in the acquisition because it thought the prospect of this transaction was unclear.

Finally, after several rounds of discussions, Apax Partner agreed to postpone the deadline for closing from January to April 2015 provided that Bright Food was required to pay the liquidated damages into an escrow account and if the closing could not be completed in three months, the liquidated damages would be transferred to Apax Partner. Fortunately, Bright Food completed the approval procedures prior to the specified date and closed the transaction as scheduled.

On June 8, 2015, Bright Dairy announced that it planned to issue up to 559 million shares to Xinsheng Investment, Shengchuang Investment, Yimin Group, SAIC Capital, Guosheng Group and Pukeyuan Fudayi at a price of RMB 16.1 per share to raise funds RMB 9 billion. Of the funds raised, RMB 6,873 million would be used for acquisition of 100% shares of Bright Food Singapore Investment Pre. Ltd. that was held by the parent company Bright Food to acquire 76.7% controlling shares of Tnuva it held, and the remaining would be used as working capital. On August 10, Shanghai Stated-owned Assets Supervision and Administration Commission approved the application for private issue of shares of Bright Dairy for the purpose of funds raising of up to RMB 9 billion. Later on August 14, Bright Dairy held the first extraordinary general meeting in that year at which the proposal for private issue of A-shares was approved. However on February 28, 2016, Bright Dairy suddenly announced to terminate the private issue of A-shares because the stock price of Bright Dairy at that time (RMB 10.76 per share) was far lower than the planned issue price (RMB 16.1 per share) and it would be unacceptable to the subscribers. On March 17, Bright Dairy announced that it entered into an escrow agreement with Bright Food International (a subsidiary of the major shareholder Bright Food) and Bright Food Singapore Investment Pre. Ltd. under which 76.7% shares of Tnuva were taken by Bright Dairy in escrow.

Case Analysis

This case mainly describes the process of Bright Food's acquisition of Tnuva. This is another milestone in the global expansion strategy of Bright Food following its acquisition of Synlait Milk, a New Zealand company.

Despite of infertile arable land and scarce water resources, Israel has a highly-developed agricultural industry and its cattle raising technology also takes lead in the world. The unit milk yield of improved cows reaches 12 tons, No.1 in the world, and the output value of cattle raising accounts for 14% of the agricultural industry. As the volume of milk imported to China increases significantly in recent years, the cooperation with Bright Food could help Tnuva sell its high-quality products in the Chinese market via the marketing channels of Bright Food, e.g. organic yogurt, cheese, fresh milk, butter, dessert, whey powder, which will finally contribute to the global development of Tnuva.

The subsidiary of Bright Food, Synlait Milk, could supply milk powder to Tnuva in the off season of milk production in Israel. Such an industrial chain among Israel, New Zealand, and China will produce strong synergy effects. As the largest dairy producer in Israel, Tnuva also has advantages in the fields such as meat and frozen food. The acquisition would integrate the technical research and development, marketing, and channel advantages of Tnuva to effectively promote the lean development of Bright Food in the whole industrial chain.

Conclusion

Bright Food's acquisition of Tnuva in Israel is a successful case of transnational direct investment, which may be taken as a model by Chinese enterprises in the global expansion under the Belt and Road Initiative. It proves that the acquirer shall engage with the major shareholders of the acquiree before the acquisition and conduct in-depth cooperation with the acquiree in international market development, product technology research and development, raw materials supply and other aspects after the acquisition to produce synergy effects. It also shows that the Belt and Road Initiative is helpful for strengthening the cooperation between China and the countries along the Belt and Road to reshape the overall pattern of overseas M&A of Chinese enterprises.

Questions

(1) What may be learned from the transnational acquisition case of Bright Food?

(2) Which legal risks may be faced by the Chinese enterprises in overseas investment under the Belt and Road Initiative?

3.5   International Investment Dispute and Applicability of Arbitration Proceeding

Related Knowledge

International investment; Convention on the Settlement of Investment Disputes Between States and Nationals of Other States (Washington Convention); International investment dispute settlement mechanism; Jurisdiction

Case Description

Saipem is a company registered in Italy and mainly engaged in oil and gas pipeline laying business. On February 14, 1990, Saipem entered into a contract with a state-owned enterprise in Bangladesh called Bangladesh Petroleum Corporation for laying of 409 km long oil and gas pipeline in Bangladesh at a total contract price of around $34 million. The project was financed by the World Bank and the International Development Association, an affiliated agency of the World Bank. Although it was required under the contract to be completed on April 30, 1991, the time of completion was delayed by one year as agreed by the two parties because of the opposition of local residents and other issues during the project duration. But Bangladesh Petroleum Corporation did not pay the advance payment to Saipem as required in the contract and the two parties failed to reach an agreement on the additional expenses of Saipem during the project delay, Saipem initiated an arbitration proceeding with the ICC International Court of Arbitration on June 7, 1993 according to the contract.

After the arbitration tribunal was formed, Bangladesh Petroleum Corporation filed a lawsuit with the court in Bangladesh on the grounds that arbitration shall not apply to the dispute according to the BIArb Arbitration rules. On November 24, 1997, the Supreme

Court of Bangladesh issued an injunction that ordered Saipem to stay the arbitration in the ICC International Court of Arbitration and on April 5, 2000, the Primary Court of Dhaka rejected the jurisdiction of ICC International Court of Arbitration. On April 30, 2001, the ICC International Court of Arbitration issued a decision to continue the arbitration and on May 9, 2003, it issued the arbitration award against Bangladesh Petroleum Corporation which required it to pay Saipem $6 million and €110,000.

After the arbitration award was issued, Bangladesh Petroleum Corporation filed a lawsuit with the local court to request revocation of the arbitration award made by the ICC International Court of Arbitration, which, however was dismissed on April 21, 2004, by the Supreme Court of Bangladesh who stated that the arbitration award of the ICC International Court of Arbitration should be void ab initio. On October 5, 2004, an application for arbitration was made by Saipem to the International Center for Settlement of Investment Disputes (ICSID) according to the bilateral investment protection agreement between Bangladesh and Italy.

Case Analysis

This case is mainly about the dispute arising from the contract between Saipem and Bangladesh Petroleum Corporation for the oil and gas pipeline laying project in Bangladesh, as well as the means of settlement and jurisdiction of the dispute. This case may be analyzed from the following aspects.

(1) Does Saipem have the right to submit the dispute to the ICC International Court of Arbitration?

(2) Does the court of Bangladesh have the right to overrule the arbitration award made by the ICC International Court of Arbitration?

(3) Is the Washington Convention applicable to this case?

(4) Is the arbitration proceeding of the ICSID applicable to the dispute in this case?

Generally, international commercial disputes may be submitted to the institutions like ICC for arbitration provided that it is agreed by the parties involved. If it was explicitly agreed in the contract between Saipem and Bangladeshi Petroleum Corporation that the dispute (if any) shall be governed by Bangladesh laws, it would be inappropriate for one party to submit the dispute for arbitration. The point in this case was that one party submitted it for arbitration and the other party sought protection from the domestic laws. In such a case, if both home countries of the two parties were member states of the Washington Convention, they may consider whether the investment fell within the scope set force in Article 25 of the Washington Conventions and whether the dispute was directly arising from the investment. Based on the merits of the case, it would be correct for Saipem to submit the dispute to the ICSID for arbitration in accordance with the bilateral investment protection agreement between Bangladesh and Italy.

Conclusion

The case may refer to the relevant provisions of the Washington Convention and the dispute may be settled by arbitration of the ICSID. The bilateral investment protection agreement between Bangladesh and Italy may also be taken as basis for the settlement of the dispute.

Questions

What is the Washington Convention and its dispute settlement mechanism and proceeding?

3.6　Applicability of the Most–Favored–Nation Treatment Clause

Related Knowledge

Transnational investment; Investment treaty; Investment protection; Most-Favored-Nation (MFN) Treatment

Case Description

An Argentine investor named Maffezini invested in and built a chemical plant in Spain and later a dispute arose between it and the local government. According to Article 10 of the 1991 Bilateral Investment Treaty between Spain and Argentina, Maffezini was required to seek judicial relief from the Spanish court before submitting the dispute for arbitration to the ICSID. But according to Article 10 of the 1991 Bilateral Investment Treaty between Spain and Chile, only consultation was required before one party (the investor) resorted to the ICSID against the other party (local government). Furthermore, Article 4 of the Bilateral Investment Treaty between Spain and Argentina stated that "the principle of most favored nation treatment shall apply to all matters under the treaty", under which Maffezini claimed the treatment listed in Article 10 of the Bilateral Investment Treaty between Spain and Chile, that is, Maffezini may submit the dispute to the ICSID for arbitration directly even it had not filed a lawsuit with the Spanish court beforehand.

Case Analysis

The case is mainly about the dispute between an Argentine investor that made investment in Spain and the local government, which mainly involves the applicability of MFN treatment and investment treaty.

1. Applicability of MFN treatment

The MFN treatment requires that the host country shall accord treatment to a foreign investor not less favorable than that which it accords to the investors of any third country, which means that each Contracting State shall in its territory accord investments and returns of investors of the other Contracting State treatment not less favorable than that which it accords to investments and returns of investors of any third State, and each Contracting State shall in its territory accord investors of the other Contracting State, as regards of the activities associated with the investment, treatment not less favorable than that which it accords to any investors of any third State with similar treaties. "Activities" associated with investment refer to the management, maintenance, use, enjoyment, acquisition or disposal of the investment.

In previous cases, the MFN clause were only applicable to the matters related to the merits of the case, not applicable to the jurisdiction and other procedural issues not falling within the scope of "similar treaties". Considering that the current dispute settlement is highly associated with the protection of investors, the MFN clause shall apply to procedural matters if the dispute clauses contained in the treaty with the third country provide more protection for foreign investors than the local relief clause in the underlying treaty.

2. Applicability of bilateral investment treaty

Bilateral investment treaties generally specify the treatments enjoyed by the investors in order to protect the interest of domestic investors. According to Article 4 of the Bilateral Investment Treaty between Spain and Argentina, MFN clause applies to all matters under the treaty. Bilateral investment treaty constitutes the direct basis for MFN treatment.

Conclusion

It is justified for the Argentine investor Maffezini to claim the treatment not less favorable than those stipulated in Article 10 of the Bilateral Investment Treaty between Spain and Chile and file an arbitration with the ICSID without filing a lawsuit in the Spanish court in advance. The MFN clause shall apply to procedural matters in the case.

Questions

Are MFN clauses applicable to procedural matters?

3.7 Huawei Suffered Discriminatory Treatment by the U.S. Administration

Related Knowledge

Transnational investment; Market entry; Discriminatory treatment

Case Description

The United States imposed its first sanction on Huawei in May 2019 by prohibiting Huawei from using the Electronic Design Automation (EDA) technology produced in the United States and the Google Maps. But Huawei was not disallowed to use the EDS already purchased in its chip design.

On May 15, 2020, the United States upgraded the level of its sanctions on Huawei's chip business by prohibiting the manufacturers using EDA technology, such as TSMC and SMIC, from supplying chips to Huawei. But Huawei could still engage a third party to produce chips or purchase chips from a manufacturer that is not controlled by the United States, such as MTK and Samsung. On August 17, 2020, the United States modified its sanction conditions again by prohibiting the companies including MTK and Samsung which produced software based on American technology from producing chips for Huawei. The cloud services business of Huawei's subsidiaries also suffered sanctions.

Moreover, the United States imposed restrictions on the acquisition activities of Huawei, prohibited Huawei from entering the US market, lobbied and threatened other countries to reject the 5G technology of Huawei and implemented technical blockage with the excuse of security. The Harmony operating system, Huawei mobile services, and Huawei software store also suffered all-round sanctions of the United States.

Case Analysis

This case describes the restrictions and sanctions imposed by the United States on Huawei, which mainly include prohibiting other countries from using Huawei technologies and prohibiting chip manufacturers from supplying chips to Huawei.

The sanctions of the United States on ZTE and Huawei started as early as in 2017. On March 22, 2017, the U.S. Department of Justice filed a lawsuit against ZTE by stating that ZTE exported source products under the control by the United States to Iran in violation of the U.S. sanctions on Iran. This led to the prohibition of SMIC from supplying chips to Huawei and constituted restraints on the development of Huawei. The common measures of economic sanctions of the United States were entity list and other U.S. sanctions lists, both based on the extraterritorial jurisdiction of the United States.

As the role of technology becomes more and more important, the United States raised the level of its sanctions on Huawei. In addition to restrictions on acquisition by Huawei, prohibition of Huawei from entering the American market, and technical blockage of Huawei technology, the United States also carried out a series of non-traditional security investigations and judicial charges on Huawei on the grounds that Huawei endangers the national security of USA, conducted negative publicity about Huawei, and imposed pressure on American enterprises and consumers to keep a commercial distance from Huawei.

The United States generally upholds the America first policy and ideas in its economic sanctions on other countries and, on the basis of primary sanctions, extends the scope of application of the restrictions to third party natural persons or entities by implementing secondary sanctions, and expands the unilateral sanctions system into a multilateral sanctions system.

The root cause for the United States to impose sanctions on ZTE and Huawei and incorporate a number of Chinese entities in the "entity list" lies in its America first policy and its ambition of maintaining hegemony. The unilateral sanctions of the United States on foreign entities by way of domestic bills and administrative orders are extraterritorial application of domestic laws of the United States in nature. Its legality is controversial in the field of international law.

Conclusion

Frictions and conflicts among countries in international issues increase with the global integration of economy and the escalation of global competition. In the wake of unilateralism and de-globalization, countries tend more to build trade barriers and technical barriers through sanctions. Confronted with such a situation, China and Chinese enterprises may take economic, legal, and development strategy measures such as list system, sovereign equality and legislation on blocking.

Questions

How to evaluate the discriminatory treatment imposed on Huawei by U.S. Administration?

3.8 Standard of Treatment of Foreign Investors

Related Knowledge

Transnational investment; Fair and equitable treatment; Sharing agreement

Case Description

The Government of Ecuador represented by Petroecuador entered into a sharing agreement on May 21, 1999 with Occidental Petroleum Exploration and Production Company, a wholly-owned subsidiary of Occidental Petroleum, for joint development of the oilfield of No.15 mining area in Ecuador. It was specified in the sharing agreement that the transfer of the rights and obligations under Article 22 of the agreement should be subject to approval by the Government of Ecuador. But Occidental Petroleum Exploration and Production Company transferred 40% rights and interests under the sharing agreement to company "A" registered in Bermuda who transferred the rights and interests to a Chinese company in turn. Therefore the Minister of Energy and Mining of Ecuador issued an "order of invalidation" to terminate the sharing agreement unilaterally.

Occidental Petroleum Exploration and Production Company made an application for arbitration in July 2006 and the dispute mainly focused on the following issues: whether the arbitration tribunal had jurisdiction, whether the transfer of Occidental Petroleum Exploration and Production Company without the consent from the Government of Ecuador was valid and whether such transfer would definitely lead to termination of the sharing agreement, and whether the Government of Ecuador's termination of the sharing agreement unilaterally violated the clauses on fair and equitable treatment and expropriation under the bilateral investment treaty between the United States and Ecuador.

The arbitration tribunal held that both the sharing agreement and the laws of Ecuador required that the transfer of the rights and obligations under the sharing agreement should be subject to approval by the Government of Ecuador, and the transfer of Occidental Petroleum Exploration and Production Company without consent was indeed improper. But the transfer without consent would not definitely lead to termination of the sharing agreement. It was not in line with the principle of fair and equitable treatment clause to punish Occidental Petroleum Exploration and Production Company by terminating the contract.

The Government of Ecuador made an application for revocation of the arbitration award in October 2012. In November 2015, the special committee of the ICSID partially revoked the arbitration award of the "Occidental Petroleum Exploration and Production Company

V.S the Government of Ecuador" case on the grounds of "ultra vires (doctrine)". The special committee held that because the first applicant Occidental Petroleum Exploration and Production Company held 60% rights and interest in the subject matter of the contract (oilfield of No. 15 mining area), the compensation for Ecuador should be reduced to 60% of the original amount claimed, that is, $1.06 billion. The remaining parts of the original arbitration award were not affected by the partial revocation.

Case Analysis

This case describes the dispute between the Government of Ecuador and Occidental Petroleum Exploration and Production Company arising from the sharing agreement between them and the arbitration results. The case involves the following clauses about transnational investment.

The fair and equitable treatment clause is frequently referred to in the arbitration on transnational investment related disputes. Except a few cases, most of the cases under arbitration of the ICSID involve the fair and just treatment clause. It is called the Empire Clause in the international investment law.

In practice, 11 violations in international investment arbitration may invoke the fair and equitable treatment clause, including violation against the due process, arbitrary and discriminatory measures, failure of protection of the legitimate expectations of foreign investors, and lack of transparency, etc.

With the continuous development of international investment and the emerging types and modes of international investment, new forms of investment disputes will appear and the conditions that would invoke the fair and equitable treatment clause will emerge.

Conclusion

Only when the fair and equitable treatment clause is strictly limited in the scope of application based on the components of international custom law, which means that the host country does not violate the proper procedure or take discriminatory acts and arbitrary measures, may the fair and equitable treatment clause be in line with the purpose of bilateral investment treaty and ensure the bilateral investment treaty is in nature the law made by the nation, not by the judge.

Questions

(1) What does the fair and equitable treatment clause generally include?

(2) Should the applicability of the fair and equitable treatment clause be limited?

Chapter 4

International Commercial Contract

4.1 Sale Contract and Anti–Dumping Duty

Related Knowledge

Import and export of goods; Sale contract; FOB; Anti-dumping duty

Case Description

The buyer (an American importer) and the seller (a Chinese exporter) entered into five sale contracts in 2015–2016 for the sale of a category of commodities. Later in the performance of contract, a dispute arose between them as the transaction was subject to anti-dumping duty in America. The buyer claimed that the commodity was subject to anti-dumping duty in America (the destination) because the seller provided the incorrect name of the importer and that anti-dumping duty should be borne by the seller. The seller argued that the trade term agreed in the contract was FOB, under which the import duties should be borne by the buyer.

Case Analysis

The dispute arising from the contract between the buyer and the seller mainly lies in who should be responsible for the anti-dumping duty.

The case is analyzed based on the arbitration award.

The arbitration tribunal held that anti-dumping duty was a tariff imposed on the commodities sold by the seller that were priced below the cost or the local market value in the export country, which affected the business of the operators of similar commodities in the importing country. The anti-dumping duty was imposed on the American importer at the time or after the commodity was delivered to the US customs. Therefore, the obligation for taxes and duties under FOB trade term should be borne by the buyer.

The seller should also be liable to a certain extent because it provided the incorrect name of the importer and failed to assist the buyer in providing relevant evidence requested by the buyer for correction. The seller breached its obligation of notification and assistance under the contract, and should be partially liable for the loss. Therefore, the arbitration tribunal ruled that the seller should bear 50% of the loss suffered by the buyer from anti-dumping duty.

Conclusion

Both the buyer and the seller are obliged to provide necessary assistance for the performance of obligations of the other party, which is required not only in the International Rules for the Interpretation of Trade Terms (INCOTERMS), but also under the principle of good faith in the commercial contract.

Questions

Compare INCOTERMS 2010 and INCOTERMS 2020 to find their similarities and differences.

4.2　A Claim Arising from Fish Meal Import Contract

Related Knowledge

International trade; Contract for international sale of goods; Risk transfer under CFR

Case Description

On March 6, 2000, a company in Qingdao (the buyer, and the plaintiff) entered into a contract for import of 5,000 tons Chilean fish meal with a company in America (the seller, and the defendant) under the trade term of CFR (cost and freight) at the price of $506.5 per ton. It was required in the contract that the fish meal delivered by the seller should not contain any live insects, salmonella and shigella as inspected at the port of shipment.

It was required to deliver 3,000 tons fish meal in April-May, 2000, and 2,000 tons in May-June 2000.

For the terms of payment, the buyer was required to make an application to the Qingdao Branch of Bank of China for opening an irrevocable L/C at sight in favor of the seller prior to March 15, 2000. The L/C shall keep valid for 35 days after the date of the B/L and the seller was required to deliver the B/L in Hong Kong before June 30. It was also required in the contract that the buyer shall procure all risk insurance according to the Institute Cargo Clauses. The documents for negotiation shall include the complete shipment inspection documents issued by a third-party inspection and identification agency and the buyer reserved the right of re-inspection at the port of destination.

The seller loaded 3,150 tons fish meal on May 31 to the Conquest vessel and submitted complete documents for negotiation in Hong Kong on June 30, which, however, were rejected because of an incorrect letter in the documents. On July 22, the Conquest vessel arrived at Qingdao port for unloading. On July 31, the buyer notified the seller by telegraph that a lot of live dermestes friscnii kugs were found in fish meal. On August 2, the fish meal was unloaded and taken into the warehouse; On August 3, the buyer notified the seller by fax for requesting the insurance policy. After the request was rejected, the buyer made a deduction of 20% of the payable amount on the grounds of fish meal containing dermestes friscnii kugs, and made a claim for $1.05 million to the seller.

Case Analysis

The case is about an import and export contract of goods in the field of international trade. The parties of the contract, quantity and standard of the subject matter, contract price, mode of payment, and terms of delivery are clear. The dispute arises from the quality of goods.

Under the trade terms of CFR, neither the buyer nor the seller is mandatorily obliged to procure insurances, the risks in the loss of or damage to the goods pass on to the buyer when the goods are on board the vessel at the port of shipment. The seller must give due notice to the buyer for the delivery of goods.

The key to the responsibility for the subject matter of the contract was risk transfer, not the quality of goods, because the seller has fulfilled the obligation of delivery by loading the goods at the port of shipment and obtaining complete shipment inspection documents which indicated that the goods met the quality requirements.

The buyer may claim against the insurer if it procured all risks insurance according to the Institute Cargo Clauses under the contract, regardless of whether the fish meal was infested due to external causes or inherent defects.

Conclusion

The rights and obligations of the buyer and the seller in the international contracts for sale of goods depend upon the trade terms they select. For the purpose of this case, the buyer's claim was unjustified.

Questions

What are the specific provisions regarding risk transfer in the international sale of goods?

4.3   Dispute from Equipment Sale and Installation Contract

Related Knowledge

Offer; Acceptance; United Nations Convention on Contracts for the International Sale of Goods

Case Description

The plaintiff: EAS, a company mainly engaged in design, manufacturing, integration, and installation of automation equipment, with the main place of business in Madison Heights in the State of Michigan, USA.

The defendant: TF, a company in Nova Scotia, Canada and headquartered in Ontario that offered heavy metal stamping parts for the customers.

EAS and TF reached an agreement under which EAS was engaged to design, manufacture and install Sport Bar system for TF. EAS sent quotations to TF on July 19, 2005 which stated that the total price for the design and manufacturing of the Sport Bar system for TF was $540,000 and the date of delivery was March 30, 2006. On the same day, TF gave an oral notice to EAS for starting the relevant work for the Sport Bar system.

On August 30, 2005, TF issued a written purchase order which contained clauses on the governing laws: the contract is concluded when the seller accepts the offer issued by the buyer to it and all matters related to contract conclusion must be governed by and construed in accordance with the laws of the place where the buyer's headquarters is registered. Any legal action in connection with the contract must be subject to the jurisdiction of the court of the province where the buyer's headquarters is registered. It meant that the disputes arising from the contract shall be governed by Canadian law.

During the design and manufacturing period of the Sport Bar system from August to October 2005, the representatives of TF held meetings regularly with EAS for the relevant issues. On October 21, 2005, the responsible person of TF gave an instruction to EAS which required EAS to deliver the Sport Bar system and complete the subsequent installation in Ontario, Canada prior to December 31, 2005.

EAS made a shipment to Canada on December 31, 2005. EAS stated that it agreed to deliver the equipment in advance because TF undertook to provide assistance for accelerating the installation of Sport Bar system. But TF did not provide such assistance while the workers of EAS were carrying out auxiliary work for the installation and test of the Sport Bar system in Ontario, where the facility was located. Later TF didn't pay the balance and the interest accrued although it was operating the Sport Bar system. Therefore, TF exercised lien on the equipment and filed a lawsuit with the local court in America to require TF to pay the remaining contract price with interest. But TF claimed that it was agreed in the contract that the dispute shall be governed by Canadian laws and it made an objection to the local court in America against the claims of EAS on the grounds of inconvenient court. The court of America held that the objection of TF should be dismissed before the governing law was finally determined.

Case Analysis

The case is mainly about the dispute between EAS (an American company) and TF (a Canadian company) arising from the contract for equipment sale, installation and payment.

The first contention was about the governing laws. EAS sent quotations to TF on July 19, 2005 which contained such information as the total contract price and the date of delivery, and on the same day, TF gave an oral instruction to EAS for commencing the relevant work of the Sport Bar system. Such legal fact indicated that the quotations issued by EAS constituted an offer and the oral instruction of TF constituted an acceptance.

On August 30, 2005, TF issued a written purchase order that contained the clause on governing laws by stating that "the contract is concluded when the buyer accepts the offer issued by the seller to it". It meant that a contract for international sale of goods was reached between EAS and TF. The dispute arising from the contract shall be governed by the United Nations Convention on Contracts for the International Sale of Goods.

The United Nations Convention on Contracts for the International Sale of Goods contains no provision on the "lien" over the contract equipment exercised by EAS. This issue should be governed by the governing laws determined according to the rules of private international law. In this case, the offer from EAS constituted an essential part of the contract. The contract was concluded and performed in Michigan, United States. Therefore, the lien over contract equipment shall be governed by the American laws on the lien over particular equipment, under which the plaintiff EAS had the right to retain the contract equipment until the defendant TF paid the remaining price with interest.

Conclusion

The conclusion of the contract between EAS (American company) and TF (Canadian company) and the dispute arising from the contract shall be governed by the United Nations Convention on Contracts for the International Sale of Goods. EAS may release the "lien" over the contract equipment after TF fulfills the payment obligations under the contract.

Questions

(1) According to the United Nations Convention on Contracts for the International Sale of Goods, which remedies are available to one party when the other party is in breach of the contract?

(2) Which provisions in the United Nations Convention on Contracts for the International Sale of Goods are applicable to the offer and the acceptance?

4.4   Risk Transfer under a Forklift Export Contract

Related Knowledge

International trade; Contract for international sale of goods; FOB; Division of risks

Case Description

A Korean company K entered into a contract with a Malaysian company M in 2019 for the export of forklifts based on the trade terms of FOB (Free on Board, Busan Port). During the loading on April 1, 2019, one forklift was damaged because it accidentally fell on the deck of the vessel during lifting. After the loading at the port of shipment was completed on April 2, the captain issued the on board bill of lading in which it was stated that except for one forklift that was damaged during loading, all other forklifts were intact and in good condition. The Korean company K also gave a notice of shipment to the Malaysian company M on that day. The forklifts arrived in Malaysia on April 15, and during receiving, Company M found that in addition to the damaged forklift indicated in the bill of lading, other forklifts also suffered surface damage such as scratches, deformation, or lamp breakage due to collision in the cargo hold. Company M then made a claim against Company K on the grounds of improper delivery of goods. Company K held that the risks of goods had been transferred after they crossed the ship's rail at the port of shipment as set force in the contract. The damage to goods occurred after they crossed the ship's rail at the port of shipment should be borne by Company M.

Case Analysis

This case is mainly about a contract for international sale of goods and the transfer of the risks in the subject matter of the contract.

According to the main provisions on the rights and obligations of the buyer and the seller under the trade term FOB, the seller is required to deliver the goods to the ship designated by the buyer at the designated port of shipment within the date or period required in the contract, and bear all costs and expenses and all risks of loss or damage of the goods before they are delivered on board. All expenses and the risks of loss or damage of the goods after loading on board shall be borne by the buyer. It is explicitly stated in the trade terms of FOB that the risk is passed on when the goods is "on board", that is, the risk of loss or damage of the goods is passed on by the seller to the buyer when the goods is loaded "on board" to the ship designated by the buyer at the port of shipment. That is to say that all risks and expenses after the loading of goods shall be borne by the buyer.

In practice, the seller must provide the "on board bill of lading" for and give the "Notice of Shipment" to the buyer, which would mean that it is agreed by the two parties that the seller has borne all the risks and expenses before the goods are loaded on board. Moreover, it is not mandatory for the buyer or the seller to procure insurance. The buyer may procure insurance at its own discretion.

Conclusion

For the purpose of this case, the seller issued the "On Board Bill of Lading" and "Notice of Shipment" after the goods were loaded on board. The damage to the forklifts (other than that indicated in the bill of lading) occurred in the cargo hold due to collision, that is, after the "loading on board" and the seller had completed its delivery obligations. Accordingly all risks and expenses after "loading on board" shall be borne by the Malaysian company M.

Questions

(1) Describe the applicability of the trade term FOB in the contracts for international sale of goods.

(2) Which specific provisions for risk transfer of goods and division of responsibilities are set force in the trade term FOB?

4.5 "Material Breach of Contract" Clause

Related Knowledge

Contracts for international sale of goods; Fundamental breach; Predictability; Delay in performance

Case Description

A buyer in Germany entered into a purchase contract for autumn clothes with a seller in Italy under which the seller was required to supply the clothes in batches from June to

September. But the seller was delayed in the performance of its delivery obligations from the supply of the first batch, and the last batch was delayed till November 10. Therefore the buyer refused to take delivery on the grounds of delayed supply (also for the previous supply). The buyer filed a legal action against the seller after the negotiation failed.

Case Analysis

The dispute in question between the buyer and the seller arose from the delay in delivery of goods under the contract. The United Nations Convention on Contracts for the International Sale of Goods shall apply to the contract because one party (the buyer) thereto is in Germany and the other party (the seller) is in Italy.

Under the United Nations Convention on Contracts for the International Sale of Goods, whether the buyer is entitled to rejection of taking delivery when the seller is delayed in delivery depends on the time of delivery as agreed in the contract, which is of legal essence.

Delay in delivery would definitely result in fundamental breach of contract in regular or seasonal trading of goods. The goods purchased by the buyer were autumn clothes for women, which was clearly aware of by the seller. The seller should predict that the buyer would be highly possible to abandon the contract if it could not receive the goods until the end of autumn.

Conclusion

According to Article 25 of the United Nations Convention on Contracts for the International Sale of Goods, it can be concluded that the seller was in fundamental breach of contract and accordingly the buyer had the right to refuse to take delivery and terminate the contract.

Questions

How to understand the "fundamental breach of contract" clause in the United Nations Convention on Contracts for the International Sale of Goods and the conditions for its application?

4.6   Rules on "Obligation of Taking Delivery"

Related Knowledge

United Nations Convention on Contracts for the International Sale of Goods; Specific performance; Obligation of taking delivery

Case Description

An equipment manufacturer in Italy (the seller) entered into a sale contract of printers with a French company (the buyer). The seller supplied the equipment according to the contract, but the buyer failed to take delivery within the agreed time and gave no reply after the seller issued a warning and granted extension for performance. The seller finally declared to terminate the contract and required the buyer to take compensation for the losses. But the buyer contended in the defense that it failed to take delivery because it had not completed its workshop for the equipment and the seller's termination of contract was in contravention of the principle of good faith.

Case Analysis

The case is about a dispute arising from the delivery of goods under the contract between the buyer and the seller. The dispute shall be governed by the United Nations Convention on Contracts for the International Sale of Goods.

Generally, the breach of the obligation of taking delivery of goods does not constitute fundamental breach of contract unless under some special circumstances. For example, it was necessary for the seller to vacate its warehouse or unload the vehicles, especially when bulk goods are supplied in which the normal production and operation of the seller depend on the buyer's taking delivery on time.

If the seller has granted additional time for performance, the seller was deemed to have fulfilled its contractual obligations and taken remedy. For the purpose of this case, the buyer neither gave reply nor took delivery after the seller granted additional time for performance of the obligation of taking delivery, which constituted a breach of the obligation of taking delivery.

Conclusion

According to the provisions of the United Nations Covention on Contracts for the International Sale of Goods on the claim of specific performance of contract and the obligation of taking delivery, the claims of the seller are justified.

Questions

How should we understand the provisions on the obligation of taking delivery in the United Nations Convention on Contracts for the International Sale of Goods?

Chapter 5

International Transportation of Goods

5.1 Application of Bill of Lading

Related Knowledge

International transportation of goods; Consignor; Carrier; Bill of Lading (B/L)

Case Description

Company A and Company B entered into a contract for international transportation of goods in July 2019 under which Company A was required to transport a batch of beer equipment of Company B from Yantian port, Shenzhen, China to Toronto port, Canada, and deliver the equipment to the consignee. It was also agreed in the contract that: (1) the freight shall be paid by the consignee directly to the account designated by Company A; (2) no direct contractual relationship was established between Company A and the consignee, and Company B shall act as the guarantor to guarantee Company A could receive the freight within the specified time; (3) Company A shall deliver complete clean on board bills of lading/telex release bill of lading to Company B after the equipment was loaded on board. But Company A, as the freight forwarding agency, did not receive the freight as agreed, and it was found that Company B was a defaulter in heavy debt.

Case Analysis

The case involves multiple legal relationships among the consignor, carrier, consignee and guarantor in the international transportation of goods, in which the following legal risks were present.

(1) Company A did not conduct an effective business investigation on Company B before it established the cooperation relationship with it, which would have helped Company A find that Company B was in bad debt. It was the first risk.

(2) It was agreed in the contract that the freight shall be paid by the consignee, a foreign company. It was the second risk. Company A had no branch in Toronto, Canada, knew little about the consignee, and did not obtain any information of and written commitment on freight payment from the consignee. The probability that Company B, the consignor, and the foreign consignee committed fraud in collusion existed.

(3) Company B was the consignor (owner) of the goods, which should also be the obligor for freight payment. Company A should have required Company B (rather than the consignee) to pay the freight under the contract, in which case Company A may retain the bill of lading or other effective documents and require the consignor to pay the freight before taking delivery. Unfortunately the consignor was just defined as the guarantor for freight payment. This was the third risk.

Conclusion

It is not advisable for the carrier or freight forwarding agency to undertake a business that is not in line with industrial practices. The best way for the carrier or freight forwarding agency to prevent loss is to control the bill of lading or other effective documents before receiving the freight. Furthermore, the carrier or freight forwarding agency should be able to identify the potential risks present in the contract terms.

Questions

What is the main cause for Company A's failure of receiving the freight as the freight forwarder?

5.2   Dispute in Freight Forwarding

Related Knowledge

Carriage of goods by sea; Freight forwarding; Customs clearance

Case Description

A consignor made an inquiry in early November 2018 to Company A for the freight forwarding agency fee for transportation of goods from Shanghai, China to Montreal, Canada. Later the consignor received and accepted the quotations from Company A, and sent the schedule of goods to be transported. Company A confirmed with the consignor that the goods to be transported contained that made of solid wood for which fumigation was necessary, and sent the receiving address in Shanghai to the consignor. The consignor paid the fumigation and commodity inspection charges of RMB 3,000 and the freight and the charges for custom declaration, barging, and terminal of RMB 34,450 to Company A. Company A completed the container gate-in, packaging, and booking.

On November 27, 2018, the goods were loaded on board and the carrier issued the bill of lading which contained such information as the consignee and notify party (both were Z3 Special Coffee Co., Ltd.), port of shipment (Shanghai), port of discharge (Vancouver), and place of delivery (Montreal). The son of the consignor was responsible for customs clearance at Montreal. On November 30, Company A sent the fumigation/disinfection certificate to the consignor, which, however, was verified later by the court and Shanghai Customs that it was not the certificate for the goods in this case. The goods arrived in Vancouver on December 23 but were rejected by Canada Border Service Agency because it was found in the inspection that the packaging materials for wooden goods were not compliant with relevant regulations and the IPPC mark was missing. After several rounds of communication of the consignor with Company A, Company A agreed that the goods may be returned to Hong Kong (the Hong Kong branch of Company A was the consignee).

On January 15, 2019, the son of the consignor paid the fees for goods inspection in Canada and return to Hong Kong in a total amount of 11,235.43 Canadian dollars. On February 19, the vessel carrying the goods set sail from Vancouver and then arrived in Hong Kong on March 12. On March 28, Company A notified the consignor in writing that if the consignor failed to confirm the return information and pay the warehousing charges of HKD 7,800 before the following day, the goods would be destroyed and the risks and responsibilities therefrom shall be borne by the consignor. On the same day, the consignor replied that it should not take responsibility for such risks and charges because the acts of Company A were improper, e.g. Company A repeatedly required the consignor to make a signature in the consignment note with blank columns, and Company A did not produce complete and compliance documents. Thereafter the goods were destroyed in Hong Kong.

According to the schedule of the goods consigned, shopping records in Taobao, and payment vouchers sent by the consignor to Company A, the value of the goods in question was RMB 85,249.1. In addition, the consignor and his son also paid other costs and expenses including attorney's fee of RMB 50,000, traveling expenses of RMB 6,706.7, accommodation expenses of RMB 3,396, notarization fee of RMB 7,080, translation fee of RMB 3,593.5 and express fee of RMB 71. The consignor and his son filed a legal action against Company A on the grounds that Company A provided false fumigation/disinfection certificate, failed to obtain the inspection and quarantine documents required by the customs agency, and failed to keep the goods properly. Their claims included: termination of the contract; return of the freight of RMB 34,450 for transportation from Shanghai to Montreal, fumigation and commodity inspection charges of RMB 3,000, freight of RMB 57,237.77 for transportation from Vancouver to Hong Kong; and compensation for the loss of goods of RMB 91,360.74, additional expenses for renovation change and loss of operating income (including heating fee and rent) of RMB 302,869.28 caused by delivery delay, attorney's fee of RMB 50,000, travelling expenses of RMB 10,105, translation fee of RMB 3,593.5, notarization fee of RMB 7,080, printing fee of RMB 825, and express fee of RMB 71.

Company A contended that: the statutory conditions for termination of contract were not met; the consignor and his son did not give due notice of the customs clearance requirements at the destination to Company A, which led to the failure of customs clearance; the consignor did not disclose the purpose of the goods and the opening time of the café, as a result of which the operating loss was unforeseeable when the contract was reached; the consignor failed to provide cooperation after the goods were returned to Hong Kong, which finally led to the destruction of the goods in the Hong Kong warehouse. It argued that it had no fault for the losses and shall not be liable for the losses claimed in the lawsuit.

Case Analysis

This is a dispute arising from the freight forwarding agency contract for transportation by sea. In similar disputes, the international freight forwarding agency often defended for its non-performance of contractual obligations on the grounds that it was not responsible for the customs clearance issues at the destination.

For the purpose of this case, the contractual obligations of the international freight forwarding agency are defined on the basis of the contract purpose. The international freight forwarding agency should be acquainted with the inspection and quarantine regulations and policies of China and the destination country to ensure the fumigation and quarantine of the goods and the packaging meet the requirements of the destination country. Where an international freight forwarding agency is in breach of the above contractual obligations, the scope of its liabilities (including loss of goods, loss related to goods transportation, expected profit loss related to the goods, and loss resulting from legal action) should be determined comprehensively based on the severity of default and whether it has taken effective measures.

The marine court ruled that as Company A was engaged by the consigner to deal with the container gate-in, packaging, fumigation, quarantine, booking, customs declaration, application for inspection and other issues related to the transportation of goods by sea, a freight forwarding agency relationship was established between them. The court dismissed the claim on termination of contract because the consignor failed to prove that Company A committed fraud in the conclusion of the contract which induced the consignor to enter into the contract against its true intention. Besides the court decided that the son of the consignor was not one party to the contract and his claims for default of the contract were unjustified.

The next moot point is whether Company A breached its obligations on fumigation and quarantine. Although the son of the consignor was in charge of the customs clearance of the goods at Montreal, Company A ought to clearly understand the inspection and quarantine related laws, regulations, and policies of China and the destination country to ensure compliance with the standards on fumigation, inspection, and quarantine of the goods and packaging and successful customs clearance. Article 4 of the Administrative Measures for Inspection and Quarantine of Wood Packaging of Exported Goods, as revised in 2018 by General Administration of Customs of the People's Republic of China, specified that wood packaging of exported goods should be treated and attached with special marks according to the quarantine and disinfection treatment methods set force therein. Company A could not prove that it obtained legal and valid fumigation/disinfection certificate for the goods and the wooden package of the goods had the special marks required by law. Therefore Company A failed to fulfill its contractual obligations for fumigation and quarantine of the goods and packaging, as a result of which the goods were rejected by the customs agency of Canada for non-compliance of wood packaging and missing of required marks and the contractual purpose of the consignor was frustrated. Company A shall be liable for the breach of contract.

Conclusion

The marine court made judged as follows: ordering Company A to compensate RMB 37,450 to the consignor for the expenses of fumigation, commodity inspection and quarantine, freight, customs declaration, barging, and port disbursement, RMB 57,237.77 for the amounts paid by the consignor in Canada, RMB 85,249.1 for the loss of goods, RMB 3,593.5 for translation, RMB 7,080 for notarization, RMB 71 for express, RMB 10,102.7 for travelling expenses and RMB 25,000 for attorney's fee; dismissing other claims of the consignor and the claims of the consignor's son against Company A. Neither party appealed. The judgment took effect.

Questions

Evaluate the judgment of the marine court based on the merits of the case.

5.3   Ship Collision Dispute

Related Knowledge

International transportation of goods by sea; Charter party; Ship collision; Hague Rules

Case Description

On March 2, 2019, the container ship *Safmarine Nokwanda* of Maersk collided with the container ship *Tianjin* of Xingqihao while berthing at the Busan Port. The accident caused serious loss to *Tianjin*. Lots of containers fell down and were even crushed and the hull structure was also heavily damaged. *Tianjin* carried lots of containers consigned by

Chinese freight forwarding agencies and owners. Before the collision, it had ever berthed at Tianjin port, Qingdao port, Ningbo port, and Shanghai port prior to arrival at the Busan Port, and was going to the Panama Canal, Kingston port in Jamaica, Savannah port, Charleston port and Jacksonville port in the United States.

Case Analysis

It was a dispute arising from improper berthing of ship at port. The liabilities shall be determined and divided according to relevant rules.

Both-to-blame collision clause is designed to preserve the protection a carrier has under the Hague Rules by giving a contractual indemnity against the cargo interests. The bill of lading or charter contract between the carrier and the owner of the goods may incorporate both-to-blame collision clause to protect the interests of the carrier granted by the Hague Rules. Under the both-to-blame collision clause, if the ship comes into collision with another ship as a result of the negligence of the other ship and any act, neglect or default of the master, mariner, pilot or the servants of the carrier in the navigation or the management of the ship, the owners of the goods carried hereunder will indemnify the carrier against all loss or liability to the other or non-carrying ship or her owners.

However, exclusion clauses are generally incorporated into the bill of lading to exempt the liabilities of the carrier resulting from the act, neglect or default of the master or mariner of the carrier in the navigation or the management of the ship, under which the owner of goods may only claim against the liable ship, rather than the carrier.

According to the International Convention for the Unification of Certain Rules of Law with respect to Collisions between Vessels 1910, if two or more vessels are in fault for the collision, the liability of each vessel is in proportion to the degree of the faults respectively committed and they shall also share partial loss of the carrying ship. In order to maintain its interest, the carrier may incorporate the both-to-blame collision clause under which the owner of the goods shall return the compensation it receives from the owner of the other ship in proportion to the degree of the fault. Policy clauses of the Institute of London Underwriters (ILU) stipulate that the loss that should be returned by the owner of the goods (the insured) to the carrier may be compensated for by the insurer.

Conclusion

For the purpose of this case, the container ship *Safmarine Nokwanda* of Maersk collided with the container ship *Tianjin* of Xingqihao, and *Safmarine Nokwanda* shall be fully liable for the loss of goods and the damage to the hull of *Tianjin*. The container ship *Tianjin* shall notify the owner of the goods promptly the damage to the containers. According to the both-to-claim collision clause, the owner of the goods may claim to the insurer after compensating the loss of the container ship *Tianjin*, if it procured insurance, or bear the compensation itself if it did not procure insurance.

Questions

Which provisions regarding the protection of the interest of the carrier are set in force in the Hague Rules?

5.4　China–Europe Railway Express

Related Knowledge

International transportation of goods; The Belt and Road Initiative; Electronic data exchange; paperless transportation

Case Description

Railway companies from China, Belarus, Germany, Russia, Poland, Kazakhstan and Mongolia agreed in 2017 to increase cooperation on international transportation through China-Europe Railway Express. They established a joint working group and held the first and second meetings in Zhengzhou (China) and Minsk (Belarus) respectively. Based on the results achieved in these two meetings, a special working group consisting of information collaboration experts from the seven countries was formed as organized by China State Railway Group Co., Ltd. (China Railway). The special working group held its first and second meetings in March and August 2018 at Suzhou and Chengdu respectively and conducted in-depth communication and extensive discussions on the key issues for the China-Europe Railway Express, such as electronic data exchange, paperless transportation, IT application, and bilateral information exchange mechanism. Later in March 2019, the special working group held its third meeting in Xi'an, China to discuss the transportation issues and future development of the China-Europe Railway Express.

Case Analysis

This case mainly describes the mechanism of efficient cooperation via China-Europe Railway Express under the Belt and Road Initiative. The operation of such mechanism has greatly promoted the international transportation of goods between China and the countries along.

1. Status quo of the application of electronic data exchange in international transportation by China Railway

Based on electronic information acquisition across the whole process of domestic and international transportation, China Railway independently developed an electronic data exchange platform for international transportation to provide bilateral message exchange services for neighboring countries, e.g. waybill information and instructions among the contracting states of Agreement Concerning International Carriage of Goods by Rail, confirmation and report of training marshaling information. Besides, China Railway entered into goods transportation electronic data exchange protocols or review text protocols with the railway companies in Russia, Kazakhstan and Mongolia (some protocols were under review), under which the working mechanism was coordinated, the work plan was drafted, and the content and technical specifications for electronic data exchange were defined. On the basis of the international transportation electronic data exchange between China and Russia, Kazakhstan, and Mongolia, China Railway will further promote the electronic data exchange with non-neighboring countries such as Belarus, Poland, and Germany to achieve full-coverage of pairwise electronic data exchange for China-Europe Railway Express.

2. Difficulties in paperless process of China-Europe Railway Express

To achieve paperless process of China-Europe Railway Express, all countries along need to work together to promote message-based electronic data exchange in the international transportation, e.g. waybill information and instructions and train marshaling. China-Europe Railway Express runs across multiple countries which involves long distance and duration and complex port operations. To realize paperless transportation, all countries must reach a consensus to overcome the key technical difficulties such as electronic signature for data sharing between bilateral countries, legal recognition of electronic signature, Internet-based information sharing security mechanism between non-neighboring countries, paperless document attachment technology, and requirements of involved countries on the paperless process.

Conclusion

Efficient collaboration among the railway corporations and customs of the countries along is necessary for the successful operation of China-Europe Railway Express. Paperless transportation and sharing of electronic goods information will greatly reduce the transportation cost, improve transportation efficiency, and significantly promote the economic development of the countries along. Moreover, China-Europe Railway Express is of great significance for improving the international transportation capacity and promoting the building of a community with a shared future for mankind. It also proved the correctness of the Belt and Road Initiative and the approach to global governance based on extensive consultation, joint contribution, and shared benefits.

Questions

Describe the role of paperless transportation and electronic goods information sharing for China-Europe Railway Express in promoting the international transportation of goods.

5.5　Division of Responsibilities under FOB Terms

Related Knowledge

International transportation of goods; Consignor; Carrier; Freight forwarding agency; FOB; Original bill of lading

Case Description

This was a dispute arising from a contract for international transportation of goods that involved multiple parties. The plaintiff was Linyi Nanyang Trade Co., Ltd. (Nanyang Trade), who consigned its goods to the defendant Panda Logistics Qingdao, Qingdao branch of the secondary defendant Panda Logistics (a freight forwarding company), for transportation. Panda Logistics Qingdao, as the agency of Panda Logistics, issued the complete original bills of lading of the goods which stated that Nanyang Trade was the consignor, Panda Logistics was the carrier, and Panda Logistics Qingdao was the authorized signatory agent of Panda Logistics.

To complete the transportation of the goods, the defendant delivered the goods to the actual carrier TS Lines for transportation, for which the consignor was Panda Logistics and the consignee was Huanya International Logistics Company (a logistics agency). For such transportation, the plaintiff paid the charges of departure port to Panda Logistics Qingdao. The goods involved in the case cost $324,055 at the time of loading. The plaintiff requested the court to order the two defendants to compensate for the losses of goods in an amount of RMB 1,977,869.69, with the interest incurred.

The two defendants argued that they did not establish a contractual relationship for transportation of goods by sea with the plaintiff. The trade term selected in this case was FOB, and the shipment booker should be the buyer (or its agent) of Nanyang Trade. Huanya International Logistics Company was suspected of theft and fraud, so the plaintiff was inevitably liable for the loss. The two defendants argued before the court that they had delivered the goods to Huanya International Logistics Company but the original bills of lading of the goods were not received, which were still held by the plaintiff. The defendants claimed that Huanya International Logistics Company was suspected of criminal offences and they had reported to the police.

Case Analysis

The case involves multiple parties of international transportation of goods and the contractual relationships among them, which may be analyzed as follows.

(1) A contractual relationship for international transportation of goods was established between Panda Logistics and Nanyang Trade. Nanyang Trade presented statements, remittance vouchers, and invoices in the first instance, which could prove that it had paid the charges of departure port to Panda Logistics Qingdao. It could be determined that Nanyang Trade delivered the goods to Panda Logistics Qingdao, and as the agent of Panda

Logistics, Panda Logistics Qingdao issued the bill of lading after receiving the goods. The original bill of lading indicated that the Nanyang Trade was the consignor.

The fact above showed that Nanyang Trade met the definition of "actual consignor" in the Maritime Code of the People's Republic of China. Panda Logistics argued that the trade term for the goods purchase contract was FOB and the buyer entrusted Huanya International Logistics Company for shipment booking, which could only prove that Nanyang Trade did not meet in the definition of contractual consignor. But as the actual consignor, Nanyang Trade was the consignor of the transportation contract and established a transportation contract with the carrier Panda Logistics.

(2) The defendant Panda Logistics shall take the responsibility for compensation. Article 46 of the Maritime Code of the People's Republic of China stipulated that the responsibilities of the carrier with respect to the goods carried in containers shall cover the entire period during which the carrier is in charge of the goods, starting from the time the carrier has taken over the goods at the port of loading and ending until the goods have been delivered at the port of discharge. During the period the carrier is in charge of the goods, the carrier shall be liable for the loss of or damage to the goods, except as otherwise provided for in this section. After the goods are transported to the port of discharging, Panda Logistics instructed the actual carrier to deliver the goods to a third party Huanya International Logistics Company while the complete original bills of lading were held by Nanyang Trade. As a result, Nanyang Trade lost its control over the goods. The act of Panda Logistics violated the provisions in Article 71 of the Maritime Code of the People's Republic of China which stipulated that the carrier shall deliver the goods against the bill of lading.

As the carrier, Panda Logistics breached its obligation of delivering the goods against the original bill of lading, as a result of which Nanyang Trade lost control over the goods under the bill of lading. Therefore Panda Logistics should be liable for the loss of Nanyang Trade, and it was not entitled to exemption of its obligations of delivering goods under the contract for international transportation of goods by sea against the original bill of lading on the grounds that Huanya International Logistics Company was suspected of theft and fraud and the information about the buyer of Nanyang Trade was untrue.

Conclusion

Based on the merits of the case and the fact stated by the involved parties, Panda Logistics should be legally liable for the loss of Nanyang Trade. The Chinese sellers and carriers should learn from the case that when the original bills of lading are issued, they may only deliver the goods against the original bills of lading to avoid legal risks, no matter whichever trade term is selected and whoever was responsible for shipment booking. Under FOB international trade contract, the seller must hold the complete original bills of lading of the goods if it waives the right to be named as the "consignor" therein. This is the minimum legal requirements for protection against the risks in international trade.

Questions

(1) Which precautions should be observed in the conclusion of the contract for international transportation of goods based on FOB?

(2) Which statutory obligations should be fulfilled by the parties in the delivery of goods against the original bills of lading?

5.6　Delivery of Goods without Bill of Lading

Related Knowledge

International transportation of goods; Freight forwarding contract; Bill of lading; Delivery of goods without bill of lading

Case Description

Chongqing ABC Industry Co., Ltd. (ABC) entered into a FOB goods export contract with the buyer in Turkey in November 2018 at a total price of $80,000 (30% as advance payment and 70% to be paid against the scanned bill of lading). After production, the buyer engaged Company D (a freight forwarding Company at Shanghai Port) to arrange for transportation. During shipment booking, ABC emphasized to Company D that the remaining contract price was not received yet and if a house bill of lading was issued, Company D should not deliver the master bill of lading to the buyer. On January 5, 2019, the buyer stated that it had observed the goods in the customs warehouse at the designation port and found that the quality of goods was non-compliant with the contract. The buyer claimed that it would not take delivery of goods and make payment unless the payable amount was reduced by 20%. Meanwhile, neither Company D nor the buyer provided evidences that the goods were still in the customs warehouse. It was unclear whether the goods were in the customs warehouse at the destination port or in the buyer's warehouse. But there was no doubt that the buyer had observed the goods before it made payment and obtained the original house bill of lading from ABC, and claimed price reduction unilaterally with the excuse of quality problem while providing none third party inspection report, and even threatened to refuse payment. It brought great risks to ABC.

Case Analysis

The dispute occurred mainly because the buyer claimed price reduction on the grounds of quality non-compliance of goods as seen in the customs warehouse, that is, before receiving the goods.

It constituted delivery of goods without the bill of lading. Company D argued that the goods were still in the customs warehouse at the designation port and under control of the freight forwarding agency, but it failed to provide proper evidence (e.g. warehousing certificate produced by customs warehouse or bonded warehouse at designation port).

The fact that the buyer claimed the quality of goods was non-compliant showed that it had observed the goods although the original house bill of lading was still held by ABC. It meant that the freight forwarding agency at the destination port unpacked the goods, or even released the goods to the buyer, without receiving the original house bill of lading. This constituted delivery without bill of lading. The responsible parties shall bear the responsibilities.

Conclusion

To prevent delivery without bill of lading, the seller may require the international freight forwarding agency designated by the buyer to enter into an international freight forwarding contract with it. Once the contract is executed, the designated freight forwarding agency shall take the responsibilities agreed in the contract and it will be more cautious and conscientious in the arrangement of international transportation of the goods to effectively prevent the risk of delivery without bill of lading. Moreover, the international freight forwarding contract can also effectively prevent the freight forwarding agency from exempting its liabilities in some acts based on the standard clauses in the bill of lading once any dispute occurs, which is more beneficial to the seller in arbitration or litigation.

Questions

How is the liability for delivery without a bill of lading determined in this case? What are the specific rules?

Chapter *6*

Payment in International Trade

6.1 Risks in the Export Settlement by Telegraphic Transfer

Related Knowledge

Payment in international trade; Western Union; Telegraphic Transfer (T/T); Telex release B/L

Case Description

In 2014, a garment exporter (Company A) in Yiwu, Zhejiang Province in China, entered into a CIF (Cost, Insurance, and Freight) garment export contract with an importer (Company B) in Nigeria at a total contract price of $20,000. It was agreed that 25% of the contract price shall be paid by T/T before shipment, and the remaining 75% to be paid after shipment against the facsimile bill of lading, both through Western Union. For the delivery of goods, telex release bill of lading was required. After Company B paid $5,000 through Western Union, Company A made shipment as scheduled in the contract and sent the copies of bill of lading by fax to Company B. Later Company B notified Company A that due to strict foreign exchange control of Nigeria on T/T (limited to $5,000), it may only pay the remaining $15,000 in three installments. After inquiring with the branch of Western Union in Yiwu Branch of the Construction Bank of China to confirm that the first installment of $5,000 had been received, Company A authorized the carrier to release the goods and then Company B took delivery of all goods immediately against the faxed bill of lading. Several days later when Company A intended to draw the $15,000 at the branch of Western Union in Yiwu Branch of the Construction Bank of China, it was notified that Company B had cancelled the telegraph transfer. Company A lost 75% of the contract payment.

Case Analysis

In this case, the exporter suffered loss due to the importer's cancellation of telegraphic transfer. It shows that in international trade payment, there are risks in the payment by telegraphic transfer and the exporter shall take protection measures against the risks.

(1) There is a risk of T/T cancellation by importer. The third-party cross-border T/T platform could complete T/T to the beneficiary's account promptly in about ten minutes, provided that the remitter is allowed to apply for cancellation of T/T at any time before the money is drawn by the payee which is not subject to the consent of the beneficiary. For the purpose of this case, Company A in Yiwu did not draw the money in time after it confirmed with the branch of Western Union that Company B had made a remittance. It created an opportunity for the fraud committed by the Company B in Nigeria. Such risks are frequently encountered by small and medium-sized trade companies.

(2) The risk was caused by the mode of payment of "T/T against faxed B/L after shipment + telex release B/L". The mode of payment by T/T after shipment against fax bill of lading imposed great risks to the exporter which required the importer to make payment by exercising its control over the goods. It must be used with the trade term that allows the exporter to designate the carrier to mitigate the risk of loss of the goods. Telex release B/L allows the importer to take delivery of the goods from the carrier by presenting the faxed copy of the bill of lading. When the exporter sends the bill of lading by fax to the importer to request payment by T/T, it creates convenience for the importer to take delivery of the goods in advance.

(3) The exporter incurs high cost for maintaining its rights and interest in small-amount export transactions. T/T via a third-party cross-border platform is generally selected in small-volume international trades. When the importer is in breach of its payment obligations, the cost for the exporter to safeguard its rights and interest according to the contract would possibly exceed the value of the trade, under which case the exporter had to waive its action.

(4) Under the mode of payment by T/T, whether the exporter could receive the payment for goods depends upon the credit of the importer. Selecting a creditable importer is the key to avoid unnecessary risks in the collection of payment. The exporter must collect information about the credit standing of the importer before entering into a contract with it. For example, the exporter may conduct a credit investigation on the importer by accessing its website, checking the information, or consulting with the account bank. For major customers, the exporter may conduct site visit or engage Sinosure to conduct a survey. The exporter is advisable to establish a database of customers based on the survey findings to contain detailed information about the customers, especially the credit limit and the track records of payment. For the customers with better credit standing, the exporter may make a concession to risks as appropriate when selecting the mode of payment, while for the customers with poor credit standing, the exporter shall take proper measures to prevent the risks.

After carrying out a survey and evaluation on the credit standing and assets of the importer, the exporter may require the importer to pay advance payment by T/T before shipment in the contract. The higher the proportion of advance payment is, the less the possibility and extent of the loss that might be suffered by the exporter. In practice, the exporter may generally require the importer to pay an advance payment at 20%-30% of the contract value. If the importer refuses to pay the advance payment by T/T without justified reasons and claims T/T after delivery of goods, the exporter must pay high attention to the potential risks and select proper trade terms and modes of transportation to mitigate the risks.

Conclusion

The risk of remittance cancellation is present in the traditional T/T by bank, while payment risk is also present in the T/T by a third-party cross-border platform. The exporter should strengthen investigation on the credit standing of the importer and establish a customer database to mitigate the risks in advance. The exporter should also require the importer to pay an advance payment at a certain proportion to the contract price to minimize possible losses.

Questions

(1) Compare the different risks confronted by the exporter and the importer when the settlement mode by T/T is taken.

(2) Understand the rules of application of the cross-border E-business platform and the relevant laws and regulations.

6.2　Selection of Settlement Mode in International Trade

Related Knowledge

Payment in international trade; Mode of settlement; Letter of credit (L/C); Documentary collection; Non-compliance of documents with the letter of credit

Case Description

Qingdao Yuanda International Trade Co., Ltd. (Yuanda) reached a textile export contract on May 10, 2020 with Almarran in Saudi Arabia. Since Almarran was a major customer which had purchased a great deal of beddings from Yuanda, Yuanda planned to select the settlement mode of forward letter of credit in the contract to offer financing convenience for the customer. Furthermore considering its own capital needs and for the safe of payment for the goods, Yuanda required Almarran to pay 30% of the contract price as deposit. Finally, it was agreed by the two parties that 30% of the contract price shall be paid by T/T as advance payment, while the remaining 70% should be paid by a 90-day forward letter of credit.

On June 10, 2020, Yuanda received the letter of credit sent from Almarran which required that the goods must be shipped by full container load and direct B/L must be issued by YangMing Marine Transport Corporation (Yangming) to indicate textile, No. of container, 20-foot container or 40-foot container, seal No., total number of packages or volumes, No. of L/C, and gross weight. These requirements would necessarily lead to non-compliance of documents with the letter of credit because there was no direct vessel between the two ports. Yuanda had no choice but requiring Almarran to modify the letter of credit. The salesman from Almarran replied that collection against L/C was also acceptable because the modification of L/C would incur high cost and the two parties had cooperated for long, and Almarran undertook to make payment for the retirement of documents.

The two parties failed to reach a consensus after several rounds of discussion. But considering that the two parties had cooperated for long and Yuanda had procured insurance with China Export & Credit Insurance Corporation, Yuanda continued to communicate with Almarran. Subsequently, Yuanda shipped the goods to Almarran after Almarran paid 50% of the remaining amount by T/T which would cover the production cost of Yuanda. Finally, Yuanda handed over the documents under the letter of credit to the bank for documentary collection due to non-compliance of documents with letter of credit and received the last batch of payment.

Case Analysis

The case was mainly about the selection of the mode of payment and settlement in the international sale of goods.

Unexpected conditions during performance caused changes in the mode of settlement. Therefore the case involved multiple modes of settlement. The buyer and the seller initially selected two settlement modes (T/T and L/C) in the contract. T/T is a type of remittance under which the payer makes payment to the beneficiary by bank using electronic means such as telegraph. It is based on commercial credit and has the advantages of simplicity, fastness, and low cost. It's an ideal choice where the two parties have established stable cooperation relationships and the importer is highly creditable. A letter of credit is a letter from a bank to the beneficiary which guarantees that payment will be made conditionally when the terms of L/C are met. The parties to the contract selected forward L/C at the onset, and then turned to collection due to non-compliance of documents with the L/C. Collection is a settlement mode whereby the exporter draws a draft with the importer being the drawee and authorizes its bank in the place of export to collect the money from the importer through its branch or agency bank in the place of import. Collection is classified into clean collection and documentary collection. The parties in the case selected the documentary collection, under which the exporter shipped the goods before the importer made payment.

Remittance is a type of settlement on commercial credit basis that relies on the credit standing of the buyer. All types of remittances might face the risk of recovery failure unless 100% amounts payable are paid in advance by T/T. In particular, the payment by T/T after delivery of goods imposes the greatest risk. Collection is also on commercial credit basis, under which the exporter, after shipping the goods, draws a bill and delivers it along with the commercial documents to the bank for collection. During the process of collection, the bank provides services instead of credit guarantee. Whether the payments for goods could be collected depends completely on the credit standing of the buyer. This mode is greatly risky when it is used alone. Letter of credit is on bank credit basis instead of commercial credit basis as the issuing bank takes the primary responsibility for payment. Letter of credit is designed to address the issues due to mutual distrust between the importer and the exporter, which is considered as a relatively safe mode of payment. But the letter of credit involves complex formalities, high cost, and strict requirements for the preparation of documents. Even if the sight letter of credit is selected, the issuing bank might deny acceptance on the grounds of the flexible clauses which are impractical or non-compliance of documents with L/C.

The exporter Yuanda had a strong sense of risk control. Firstly it adopted the settlement mode of "T/T (advance payment) + forward L/C" in the contract. Because Almarran required the forward settlement mode as a long-term customer and considering that L/C was a relatively safe settlement mode in international mode, Yuanda selected forward L/C instead of any other mode featuring payment after delivery of goods and required 30% of the contract price as advance payment. Secondly in the performance of contract, Yuanda selected the "T/T (partial payment) + collection" mode when it encountered non-compliance of documents with L/C. When the importer refused to modify the L/C, Yuanda required the importer to pay 50% of the remaining amount by T/T, thus ensuring its production cost was covered. That is to say, Yuanda would not suffer loss in this export transaction even if the last batch of payment could not be received.

Conclusion

There are many modes of settlement that may be selected in the international trades, including remittance, collection, letter of credit and international factoring. No one may guarantee absolute safety. The enterprises may combine any of them and procure export credit insurances according to their business needs. The modes of settlement must be suitable to the trade conditions in the contract. The seller must select the mode of settlement and take control over the settlement risks by giving due consideration to the credit standing and asset conditions of the buyer.

Questions

(1) Analyze the influencing factors in export trade risks.

(2) Compare the different settlement modes in international trade and their risks.

6.3　Rules on Letter of Credit

Related Knowledge

Payment in international trade; Letter of credit; Compliance with each other among documents; Compliance of documents with letter of credit

Case Description

Company A in Shanghai, China entered into a sale contract of electronic products with Company B in America in March 2019 at a total contract price of $100,000 and under the trade term of CFR NEW YORK BY AIR. The two parties selected irrevocable letter of credit at sight for payment and agreed to transport the goods to New York by air in the following month.

After the contract was executed, Company B opened a letter of credit in New York in which a bank in Shanghai was both the advising bank and the negotiating bank and the trade term was CNF NEW YORK. Company A consigned the goods according to the contract after receiving the letter of credit and prepared the documents required under the letter of credit for negotiation. When the negotiating bank sent documents to the issuing bank in New York, it received a denial notice from the issuing bank who stated that the documents were not compliant with the letter of credit, in particular, the trade term in the commercial invoice of Company A was CFR NEW YORK, while that in the letter of Credit was CNF NEW YORK. Company A made an objection to the issuing bank immediately and required Company B to make payment for the goods or take compensation according to the contract. Meanwhile, Company A Contacted the carrier to withhold delivery of the goods. But it was too late and the goods had been delivered. Company B refused to make compensation, while the issuing bank in New York denied acceptance of the letter of credit on the grounds of non-compliance of documents with letter of credit. Company A suffered a huge loss.

Case Analysis

This is a typical case resulting from non-compliance of documents with letter of credit. The trade term indicated in the commercial invoice was CFR NEW YORK, while that in the letter of credit was CNF NEW YORK, as result of which the issuing bank of the importer dishonored the letter of credit and the exporter suffered huge economic loss.

The letter of credit has three characteristics: (1) independence of the transaction underlying it. The letter of credit is issued on the basis of, but standards independent of and not bound by the sales contract between the importer and the exporter; (2) dealing with documents. The bank makes payment as long as the documents are compliant with each other and with the letter of credit; (3) the bank provides credit as a third party, which is in no way substantially concerned with the buyer or the seller. The bank makes payment as long as the documents are in compliance with each other and with the letter of credit as required in UCP600, regardless of whether or not the documents are within the validity or the goods are delivered to the place of import. Non-compliance of documents with the letter of credit was just the direct cause for the loss of Company A. It did not review and verify the documents against each other and the letter of credit issued by Company B, and therefore suffered great economic loss.

The exporter was unfamiliar with the rules on the trades by airway. Different modes of transportation and different trade laws and regulations impose risks to the importer and the exporter. Company A in the case suffered irreparable loss because it was unfamiliar with the characteristics of the trade by airway, applicable laws and regulations, and the process of settlement of letter of credit under air transportation. In addition, Company A adopted the standard trade term CFR while Company B adopted the past trade term CNF, which were identical in nature despite of different expressions of cost plus freight in different stages. Company A did not give due consideration to the differences between them although even a minor difference might cause huge economic loss.

Conclusion

In the practices of the payment in international trade, the issuing bank should carefully review the letter of credit, and the exporter should also review the documents against the letter of credit once receiving it, in order to ensure compliance with each other and with the letter of credit. The importer and the exporter shall also be familiar with the characteristics and applicable rules of each mode of international transportation of goods.

Questions

Analyze the legal characteristics and trading rules of letter of credit.

6.4　Standby Letter of Credit and Obligations of Payment of Issuing Bank

Related Knowledge

Standby letter of credit; Issuing bank; Applicant; Beneficiary; Draft; International Standby Practice (ISP98)

Case Description

An English bank (Bank A) issued a standby letter of credit in favor of a Japanese company (Company C) at the request of the applicant (Company B), which required the beneficiary to draw money in four installments with four drafts and provide the following applicant default statement at the time of drawing money: because the applicant (Company B) failed to pay the amount specified in one of the four bills to the beneficiary (Company C) by the date of maturity, the amount of the bill drawn shall represent the amount payable but not paid yet by the applicant.

For the first three installments, the applicant (Company B) made payments directly to the beneficiary (Company C) by the date of maturity of installments stated in the standby letter of credit, and accordingly, it was unnecessary for Company C to draw special bills under the standby letter of credit. When the fourth draft became mature, the applicant failed to make payment as scheduled, so the beneficiary submitted the default statement and draft required in the standby letter of credit to the issuing bank to demand the amount payable by the applicant against Bank A under the standby letter of credit. But Bank A rejected after receiving the documents.

Case Analysis

The case involves the issuing bank, applicant, beneficiary, and two international practices with respect to the standby letter of credit. The dispute arose mainly because the two international practices focused on different aspects.

(1) UCP600 is mainly applicable to the ordinary commercial letter of credits in the trade. According to article 32 of UCP600, if a drawing or shipment by installments within the given periods is stipulated in the credit and any installment is not drawn or shipped within the period allowed for that installment, the credit ceases to be available for that and any subsequent installment.

(2) ISP98 provides for separate rules applicable to standby letter of credit. Standby letter of credit is on bank credit basis which may be taken as means of compensation for the beneficiary in the case that the applicant is in default.

Conclusion

Since the parties in the case did not specify the governing practices of standby letter of credit, the International Standby Practices (ISP98) should prevail, under which Bank A should perform the obligations of payment.

Questions

Which rules apply to the standby letter of credit in the payment in international trade?

6.5 Payment in International Trade and UCP600

Related Knowledge

Payment in international trade; Freely negotiable letter of credit; UCP600

Case Description

On July 22, 2008, the Xiamen branch of a Chinese joint-stock bank listed in Hong Kong Stock Exchange issued a letter of credit for $8,235,000 in favor of a Singaporean trading company (the beneficiary) at the request of a buyer of Xiamen. The underlying contract was a sale contract of 45,000 WMTs (Wet Metric Tons) (+/−10% at seller's option) of iron ore fines at $183 per DMT (Dry Metric Ton) CFR/FOB. The credit was freely negotiable and was subject to UCP600. But it was stipulated that the payment be made in Xiamen 90 days after presentation.

The Beneficiary had 44,500 WMTs goods with value of $7,185,105.43 shipped from India to Mainland China on July 19 and 23, 2008 respectively. The goods arrived at Fangcheng Port on August 2 and were discharged the following day. The Beneficiary presented the documents to the negotiating bank and requested payment from the latter on July 30. On August 4, the negotiating bank delivered documents to the issuing bank who received the documents on August 6.

Later the issuing bank sent three SWIFT messages on August 11, 12, and 13 respectively. In the first message, the issuing bank accepted the documents and agreed to make payment. However in the latter two messages, the issuing bank denied the content in the first one and rejected payment in the third message on the grounds of non-compliances in the documents submitted by the beneficiary. The first alleged discrepancy was relating to the amount of the payment. The amount specified in the credit was $8,235,000 while the amount required by the beneficiary was $7,185,105.43, which had gone beyond the credit amount (+/−10%). The alleged second and third discrepancy related to the quantity of the goods. The credit required "45,000 MTs (+/−10% at seller's option)" goods to be delivered. The issuing bank alleged that 45,000 MTs should be 45,000 DMTs (as opposed to 45,000 WMTs), while that in the documents was 44,500 WMTs, equivalent to about 40,017.50 DMTs, beyond the range of +/−10% of 45,000 DMTs required in the credit. The alleged fourth discrepancy concerned the value of the goods. It was said by the issuing bank that the adjustment of value of goods shipped was outside the range of +/−10% even after the adjustment of value. On August 14, the negotiating bank, on behalf of the beneficiary, refused to accept the reasons for the rejection stated by the issuing bank. However, the market price of iron ore fines fell during that period. The seller was forced to agree with the buyer on a reduction of the unit price from $183 per DMT to 128 per DMT. The total value of goods was reduced to $5,122,240. Both parties signed on the memo of price reduction.

After suffering such losses, the Singaporean beneficiary sued the issuing bank in the High Court of Hong Kong. It contended that the latter two messages had no legal effect, so that the issuing bank could not rely on them to negate the effect of the first message which had accepted the documents and promised to pay. As a result, the beneficiary claimed for the difference between the originally agreed amount specified in the credit and what it eventually received, namely $2,062,865.43.

The issuing bank defended that it had sufficient reasons to reject the documents. It also contended the proceeding should be stayed for forum conveniens on the ground that none of the concerned parties was resident of Hong Kong and the related transactions happened in Mainland China and Singapore.

On May 3, 2010, the High Court of Hong Kong held that the issuing bank did not give a sufficient notice of refusal of payment and should pay the damage the beneficiary incurred.

Case Analysis

The dispute occurs because the beneficiary of the letter of credit suffered losses. The issuing bank and the beneficiary made different claims and demands, while the claims of the beneficiary were supported by the High Court of Hong Kong. The case may be analyzed as follows.

(1) The beneficiary argued that Articles 14, 15, and 16 of UCP600 should apply to the case. The High Court of Hong Kong also referred to these articles in detail. The judge noticed that the issuing bank sent three messages. The judge held that once the first message had accepted the documents and agreed to pay, the issuing bank shall be bound by that message to fulfill its obligation to honor the letter of credit to the beneficiary. The issuing bank can only give a single notice indicating its refusal to honor and the discrepancies.

(2) The issuing bank contended that there was only one notice of refusal, the third message sent on August 13, which listed all discrepancies and was sent within five banking days during which period the bank was entitled to determine whether the presentation complied with the credit as stipulated by Article 14 (d) of UCP600.

(3) The decision of the High Court of Hong Kong: the judgment rejected the issuing

bank's application of staying the proceeding and awarded the beneficiary the difference of $2,062,865.43 together with interest at the rate of "US prime rate plus 1% from November 9, 2008 until the date the judgment was issued" and that is applicable to the enforcement period thereafter.

Conclusion

The issuing bank made obvious errors in the formalities of document presentation, document review and dishonor, all of which brought potential risks to the issuing bank and the applicant. It is essential to accurately understand and apply the rules of UCP600, especially the interpretations of articles 14, 15 and 16 therein.

Questions

(1) Describe the basic content of UCP600.

(2) Analyze the position and roles of UCP600 in payment in international trade.

6.6　Payment in International Trade and International Factoring

Related Knowledge

Payment in international trade; International factoring; Import factor; Export factor; Documents against acceptance (D/A)

Case Description

Ronghua Household Appliance Co., Ltd. (Ronghua) in China entered the Colombian market of Latin America in March 2013 when it was negotiating with Costa Porto (Costa) for the export of electromagnetic kitchenware. Costa proposed the settlement mode of D/A at 90 days, which, however, was unacceptable to Ronghua because it was too risky and the term of payment was too long for the first cooperation between them. However, as Ronghua was highly interested in the Latin American market, it proposed international factoring. Later Ronghua applied to a branch of Bank of China in Guangdong Province for import factoring and the Bank of China selected a bank in Colombia as the import factor.

On April 20, 2013, Ronghua executed a disclosed non-recourse export factoring agreement with Bank of China and an export contract of $250,000 with Costa, after it was granted a credit line of $280,000 by the import factor. On April 28, Ronghua applied to the export factor for financing after shipment, and the export factor prepaid $200,000 to Ronghua. On July 28 when the period of payment matured, Costa sent a quality dispute notice through the import factor and rejected payment on the grounds of quality problems, which was deemed as a trade dispute by the import factor to release its bad debt guarantee obligations. Bank of China gave notice of the dispute to the exporter immediately for settlement by the importer and the exporter through negotiation. Ronghua required Costa to provide quality inspection documents, which Costa failed to provide. Ronghua thought that the reasons for the rejection of payment were unjustified. Through further investigation, it was found by Ronghua that the actual reason for rejection was that the distributor of Costa was bankrupt and the goods were attached, as a result of which Costa could not recover the payments for the goods. Within 90 days' indemnity period since the date of maturity in the invoice, the import factor failed to make payment. Bank of China required Ronghua to return the advance payment, which was refused by Ronghua who argued that it had sold the invoice and other documents to Bank of China and Bank of China should be responsible for the non-payment of the importer. On December 5, 2014, the exporter entrusted the import factor to sue the importer in Colombia. But the export factor was very negative in assisting the exporter in the settlement of the dispute. The exporter was defeated at last, and both the exporter and the export factor suffered losses.

Case Analysis

The case describes the dispute in the payment of trade between the importer and the exporter, which mainly involves the basic links of international factoring, the risks faced by the exporter and export factor, and the responsibilities undertaken by the importer and the import factor.

1. Risks

In this case, the importer alleged that the quality of goods was non-compliant and refused to make payment accordingly. The import exporter deemed it as a trade dispute which released its debt guarantee obligations. Bank of China and Ronghua entered into a non-recourse factoring agreement under which the export factor may recourse to the creditor (exporter) when it was not paid by the import factor by the date of maturity of the accounts receivable. If the export factor did not agree with the exporter on the right of recourse under the trade dispute in advance in the factoring agreement, the export factor would bear the risk of payment rejection. In this case, the exporter failed in the negotiation with the importer on quality problems and lost in court, and finally suffered losses for its failure of receiving the remaining payments.

2. Quality dispute

The buyer and the seller did not reach a consensus on whether the goods had quality problems which resulted in the trade dispute. Costa argued that the goods had quality problems but it failed to provide quality inspection certificate. On the other hand, Ronghua found that the reason for the importer's refusal of payment was that its distributor was bankrupt, as a result of which the importer could not receive the payment for the goods. While the quality problem was not verified yet, the import factor identified the trade dispute and exempted its bad debt guarantee liability by relying upon the statements of only one party. It can be seen that the importer was likely to have defects in its performance defect, and hence the exporter and the export factor suffered the risks.

3. Responsibilities of the import factor

As the agent ad litem of the exporter, the import factor was passive in assisting the exporter in the litigation. It was obvious that the import factor was not desirous of winning the litigation because once it won, the importer would be obliged to make payment. Considering that the importer was insolvent, it was highly possible that the import factor would have to bear the responsibility for the loss in the end. The import factor paid more attention to its interest than its credit, which showed that the import factor was in bad credit and could not fulfill its obligations properly as a factor.

The analysis above showed that trade dispute was a major risk in the international factoring business. All involved parties, especially the exporter and the export factor, should take precautions against the risks of trade disputes.

Conclusion

International factoring was originally intended to address the issues that affect the trades and exchanges due to mutual mistrust in the international trade of goods to reduce the risks of the exporter in foreign exchange collection and secure financing. If the exporter and the export factor fail to take proper measures for the credit risks in advance, the risk of refusal of payment by the importer would be probable. Therefore, even if the exporter selects international factoring in the settlement, risk mitigation measures shall be taken. Caution is the parent of safety.

Questions

Which legal risks are present in the international factoring business?